Spring Cleaning
for the
Soul

~Love Lessons for Life~

An inspirational guide to
finding success, happiness and abundance
right where you are!

Joy Krause

Abbondanza! ❀ *Miami*

Spring Cleaning for the Soul
~Love Lessons for Life~
An inspirational guide to finding success, happiness
and abundance right where you are!

Joy Krause

Published by Abbondanza!
P.O. Box 220173 • Hollywood, FL 33022-0173
(954) 927-3960 • FAX (954) 927-3068 • (800) 791-8799
E-Mail: SprngClng@aol.com

Publisher's Cataloging-in-Publication
(Provided by Quality Books, Inc)

Krause, Joy.
    Spring cleaning for the soul : love lessons for life : an
inspirational guide for finding financial and spiritual abundance
right where you are / Joy Krause. -- 1st ed.
    p. cm.
    Preassigned LCCN: 97-93535
    ISBN: 0-9657864- 4-7

    1. Self-help techniques--Anecdotes. 2. Success--Psychological
aspects--Anecdotes. 3. Spiritual life--Anecdotes.   I. Title.

BL632.K73 1998   158.1
                            QBI97-41064

Cover design: Arunski & Associates
Ilustrations: Dick Mahoney
Editor: Barbara Lehman

This book is dedicated with love and gratitude to:

My daughter, Kimberly: *You are my role model of courage,
creativity and compassion.*

My son, Mark: *You are my role model of adventure,
wisdom and sensitivity.*

*I love you both up to the sky, down to the ground,
and all around the world.*

And to my late husband, Eric: *You taught me how
to laugh and play.*
I will always carry you in my heart.

— Acknowledgments—

The stories in *Spring Cleaning for the Soul* were written during my many years in the home-cleaning business. They were gleaned from the lives of my customers and cleaning buddies. I wish to thank all of you collectively for allowing me into your homes and hearts.

Thanks mostly to my two children, Kimberly and Mark, and my son-in-law, Salvo: Your belief in this book and in me gave me the courage to share my heart and soul, and to hang in there until the last dust mote danced away in the light.

To Brian Jones, tap dancer and graphic artist extraordinaire: Some day when I grow up, I want to be just like you.

To Joe Arunski—thanks for a brilliant cover & design; Dick Mahoney—your illustrations captured the spirit of the characters beautifully. And to best buddy, "Jelly Fingers" Lehman aka Barbara Lehman, editor—thanks for dusting out the corners and bringing in the light.

To James Woods, Actor—You came into my life for only a moment, yet that moment illuminated previously untouched reservoirs of self-awareness and inspiration.

To my friends at the National Speaker's Association, especially Mikki Williams and Rosita Perez: Thanks for always being there with hugs and friendship.

To my proofreading pals, Cindy Ames, Roger Cousineau, Janet Cowan, Jeanne DeQuine, Jeannette Isabella, Sheila Kelly, Betsy Lampé, Howard and Mavis Salus: I never realized a page could hold so much red ink. Thanks for your kind critiques.

Finally, thank you to the Great Creative Force that nurtured these stories in my memory and helped them emerge from my soul.

Spring Cleaning for the Soul

"...They were pleasant spring days, in which the winter of man's discontent was thawing as well as the earth, and the life that had lain torpid began to stretch itself."

—HENRY DAVID THOREAU

—Introduction—

During my 20-year career, I have visited hundreds of homes. I've cleaned for households run by two men, one woman, foster parents, adoptive parents and surrogate parents. I've been paid with alimony checks, rubber checks, credit cards, checks from hidden bank accounts, with food stamps, funny money, and a few times, with dirty money.

I've watched some of my customers change locations, lovers, last names or careers. I've even watched one of my customers, Lillian Lutweigler, former data processing clerk at Thermidoro's Plumbing Supply Center, change all four at the same time when Lillian became a lunch time exotic dancer at the Foxy Dame.

I've cleaned for priests, war heroes, taxidermists, rich people who went broke and broke people who became rich. I've cleaned funeral homes, lighthouses, haunted houses and everything in between and under a roof. I've been a psychologist, spy, scapegoat and confidante. Because dirt never goes away for long, my business grew until it became one of the largest of its kind in the Northeast.

Also during those years, I was diagnosed with a tumor the approximate size of an orange. I was scared. During the next 30 days, I hired a manager to run the company while I went home to regroup. I thought about other dreams I'd had and had never gotten around to. One of them was writing, so I immediately started a journal. By the time the doctors removed the tumor, I had committed myself to this book.

A few years later I took some time off to become a cabaret singer in New York City. Well, truth be told, my specific goal was to sing *It Had To Be You* while draped across a grand piano in a gold lamé dress with a slit up to there. One year later, I was performing every Saturday night in a little club called Don't Tell Mama on West 46th and 8th in Manhattan. Go figure.

How did I get there? Here's how it happened: In the 1960's, marrying right after high school was almost obligatory, or at least I thought so. I left my home in Rhode Island and hopped a bus for California. I figured it didn't matter what century we were in: a woman needed a man and California was the place to search.

I found a small college in Orange County, where the guy-to-gal ratio was 4 to 1 and signed up. I surveyed the available pickings and immediately threw a coming out party for myself. The invitation list was predominantly male. That night 20 guys came and brought their friends.

Music was blaring and beer was sloshing. About 11 p.m. there was a loud crash at the front. A group of non-collegiate crashers had kicked in the door. Everything stopped. Eyes turned to the open doorway. There, leaning against the frame with the door knob dangling from his hand, was one of the most incredible hunks of maleness I had ever seen. Tight Levi's, cowboy boots, T-shirt with the sleeves rolled up, slicked-back hair and little boy grin.

It was the grin that finally did me in. We were married 30 days later in front of a Justice of the Peace in Las Vegas. I was 18; He was 19, and his name was Eric.

For the next eight years our party partied on, taking us from the California desert to Louisiana's oil barges and through every pool hall along the way. We danced in the moonlight. We sang *Hound Dog* in two-part harmony. We made love in every state, in every way. We were the loves of each other's lives. He was my Prince Charming.

God also blessed us with a son and daughter, Mark and Kimberly. But in 1975 things we had danced around came crashing in on us. It turned out we were children having children. He loved those kids, but he couldn't stop drinking long enough to settle down. We said goodbye in 1975 and he eventually died of alcoholism.

The split meant that, at age 27, I became mommy *and* daddy and, although I didn't know it at the time, a modern-day Cinderella. With no husband, no job, no training or education, no money and two babies, my career options were rather limited: welfare or house cleaning. I put an ad in the local paper:

Cleaning lady for hire. Windows included.

I figured it would be best to include everything. After all, what would the world have been like if Mr.

Tiffany had said, "I don't do windows?" Or, for that matter, imagine Michelangelo announcing, "I don't do ceilings."

Every day I'd load the vacuum, mop, broom and cleaning bottles into the back of our old pickup, and the kids and I would bounce along from house to house. Kim watched Mark while I scoured and scrubbed.

I discovered that I liked this world where things were simple: dust and soapy build-up were the enemy and Mr. Clean was the hero. And best of all, the cast of characters (my clients) enriched my life from that day forward.

It was Mrs. Avadesian who helped me discover that even house-cleaning can open a doorway to the soul. She was a 95-year-old widow who lived all alone in a rambling old Victorian home on the edge of town. Every other Wednesday at 9 a.m., I'd haul my cleaning equipment over there to dust and polish for two hours while she rocked in her chair, quietly observant. One day, quite by accident, I discovered that Mrs. Avadesian loved Elvis. From then on, we were Wednesday morning dance partners, and both our lives were changed.

I knew then that my work had a far greater purpose than simply scrubbing and sweeping. I was not only to help people by cleaning, but also by being present and caring. Cleaning my clients' dirty homes merely gave me an excuse to have a front-row seat in their lives. Working as a cleaning lady blessed me with an abundance of life wisdom. The keys that unlocked my customers' homes opened to far greater places of adventure and learning than any of us had anticipated.

We became each other's trusted servants, and along the way, shared confidences, pain, life experiences and spiritual maturity.

As I scrubbed and shined, the stories in this book were created wherever and whenever inspiration struck. They were written on little pieces of toilet paper, sticky-notes, and on the backs of envelopes. They were written on my heart.

They are about life, its absurdities, its bliss and its heartaches, as seen through my private cleaning-lady eyes. I've found that life is sublimely simple, yet inordinately complex. What a gift I've had over the years to witness it all first hand, as life embraced and transformed my customers and, in the witnessing, transformed me.

I finally sold the company last year and went to live in Miami Beach near my daughter, Kimberly, now 25. She is married to a Sicilian hunk named Salvo, whom she met in a supermarket. They own a paint-your-own-pottery studio and wine bar in the funky Art Deco district of Miami Beach and gaze at each other the way her dad and I did so many years ago.

Mark is a junior at Colorado State University. He lives off campus with his golden retriever, Home Run, and is blowing away his teachers with his writing. Last year he ran a carpet cleaning company out of the fraternity house. He spends his vacations sitting in rain forests or wind surfing all over (literally) the world. He has his father's gypsy spirit, extraordinary good looks and, oh yes, that little boy grin.

When I asked Mark and Kimberly if it was okay to use their real names, they said, "We'll let you know when we've read the book." They read it and gave me four thumbs up. The other names have been changed so that no one knows whose doors my ring of keys unlocked.

This life has been quite a journey, so far. I hope you will walk with me into the homes of the people I've worked for, and the people I've worked with. I'd like to share with you the discovery I made: Love & Service go hand-in-hand.

I invite you to try some spring cleaning for yourself. Throw open the windows, let in the light, and sit somewhere quiet at day's end reflecting on the people and stories in this book. I think you may find many similarities with your own life story, and that the truths revealed and the lessons learned are universal—regardless of your station in life.

So, right now, just sit back and relax, because soulful spring cleaning will take you on a wondrous journey.

Joy Krause

"It is not the critic who counts; not the man who points out how the strong man stumbled. The credit belongs to the man who is actually in the arena, whose face is marred by dust and sweat and blood."

– THEODORE ROOSEVELT

My cleaning career began with overflow: Too many bills overflowing the shoe box I had stuffed them in, and too many of my son's diapers just plain overflowing. Then there was my despair and my tears. Each morning as I piled cleaning supplies into my car, it seemed like my destiny was in the control of a string mop, an upright vacuum and a bright yellow plastic pail.

Each day I awkwardly followed strangers as they gave me the grand tour of their dusty, dirty, and sometimes dingy homes. They would rattle off a few instructions and a lot of excuses.

My new clients included working mothers, scrambling to jam careers, husbands and children into days that started too early and ended too late, all the while lamenting their inadequacies as homemakers. Emily Post's standards had created a mother-lode of guilt for these women.

Then there were the proud older folks, struggling not to relinquish their one last vestige of independence, sitting quietly as I stripped their soiled sheets from the bed.

And newly single men, with no clue about house-cleaning, who finally realized that shorts thrown on the bedroom floor would never again, as if by magic, find their way into the washing machine.

At first, it wasn't easy being privy to strangers' habits and hygiene. It's like I imagined it would be showing up naked for a blind date: embarrassing at first, but after a while, perfectly natural.

As I got to know my clients, the awkwardness passed. I was amazed to realize that beneath each person's dirty laundry, there was a heartfelt story. That grime was camouflage, layers that covered the trea-sures of someone's life. For some reason I had been cho-sen to be present at the unveiling.

Then something strange occurred. I began to see the light. Not much at first, mind you. Mostly I felt dark, despairing of my dashed hopes, doubtful of how my children and I would survive. But random rays of light would occasionally break through like an unexpected and gradual dawning in an inky night.

Why does light, disguised as "Ah ha's," come into our lives at the most unexpected times? Times when we've been dragged, kicking and screaming, down unwelcome paths only to find, in the end, it was exactly where we needed to be. (How did the Rolling Stones say it? "You don't always get what you want, but if you try sometimes, you just might find, you get what you need.") In any case, Grace was raining down on me, but I was running around blindly groping for an umbrella.

Than the "Ah ha!"

Maybe the messes I had been called to clean up were

above and below the surface. I could polish veneers with lemon oil and elbow grease, and on the other hand my loving presence could somehow return the luster to a tarnished soul.

But I told you—this was a gradual dawning. At first I thought, "Great. Just what I needed. More responsibility." Where was this new light's reset button? And how in blazes was I supposed to help shine another person's soul? It seemed to me that if I had been entrusted with the polish, I needed to apply some to my own soul. Somehow, right then, the world supply seemed scarce. I would ask myself if, when the going gets rough, those who've had it rough get a cleaning lady, who the heck does the cleaning lady get?

More about that calling...I had been called upon all right, but like most of Life's important messages, this call was dropped in my lap with no return number. I couldn't dial for further information. It was like being given the latest high-tech phone with no operating manual, no instructions, no warranty!

So, not knowing what else to do, I just kept showing up, day after weary day, scrubbing those floors, degreasing the stoves, bouncing from room to room, house to house. Soon the whole neighborhood seemed to be sparkling. Kitchens twinkled, bathrooms shone, and word of the new cleaning lady in town spread faster than grape jelly on a toddler's fingertips.

My days were jammed with new clients, each with a friend, co-worker or relative whose homes also needed scrubbing, spiffing and shining. I'd awaken before dawn to dress and feed the children. Then I'd pack the coloring books, playpen, snacks, lunches and cleaning supplies, jam them all in our old Chevy pick-up, and off we would go to the "early" jobs. (Yes, all that stuff was just for the first half of the day!) At 2:30 I'd drop the kids back at our house and a high school girl would watch them while I finished my mid-day assignments.

About 7:00 p.m. my body was more beaten than an old rug getting the dust whacked out of it. I'd drag myself home, shower, throw together some dinner, and get ready to do it all over again the next morning.

The months whirled by, soon becoming years—first one, then two. Anger gradually bubbled up pushing aside the weariness. By the third year it was at a fast simmer. Finally, self-pity boiled over and I raged at responsibility, motherhood and God. The light I'd glimpsed so long ago, some hint at a higher purpose, was flickering and threatened to extinguish itself.

What did it all mean, anyway? Life had angered me, exhausted me. Caring for the children had become a burden. Was life supposed to be a non-stop marathon just to pay the bills still overflowing the shoe box? By this time I needed more than shoes and the box they came in. I needed hip boots to wade through all the dirt and despair, and I figured that the boot box would come in handy for the ever-increasing pile of bills. As you can probably tell, I was about to throw in the dirty towel.

Then God called back. The flickering light rekindled, caught fire, and finally blazed with a healing warmth.

1

Finding Diamonds in the Dust

My life had become an endless stream of errands and responsibilities, with little or no time for me. I complained a lot until I cleaned a little ranch house in the suburbs. That's when I learned to do more hugging and less tugging with my children.

"Where's Daddy?" three-year-old Kimmy asked one morning, rubbing her eyes.

I was sitting at the kitchen table feeding her eight-week-old brother, Mark. Before answering, I imagined people in therapy recalling how they first learned of a parent's abandonment. I didn't want Kimmy to wind up there. I couldn't bring myself to tell her that Daddy had a drinking problem. How could I explain that Daddy left because he had a disease, not because he didn't love her? So, barely out of childhood myself, I began...

"Help me, Lord," I prayed, silently. "How do I tell this beautiful child that Daddy's gone?"

"Daddy went on a long trip," I said, lamely.

"Will he come home soon?" she asked, hugging my leg.

"I don't know, honey."

So began my venture into single motherhood. The children adjusted slowly, as children do, reserving their questions for Christmas and birthdays. "Do you think Daddy will call?" they would ask.

In the first grade, Kimmy designed her own interpretation of a Mother's Day card. On the cover was a crayoned picture of three stick people with orange heads and purple bodies, holding hands and smiling. Inside, on wide-lined paper, she scrawled a description of me.

> *My mommy has black hair. She cleans the house a lot and doesn't sleep much.*

She was correct about the black hair and sleep patterns, but slightly off when it came to just how many houses I was cleaning. But she was right about one thing. I worked a lot. Just at the time the kids needed me most, I had to work harder and harder.

"Quite an arm on that boy," my uncle Jack said one day as he lobbed a softball to Mark in the front yard. "Isn't it about time you checked out Little League?"

"Uncle Jack," I said, "he's four years old."

"Can't start 'em too early," he went on. "It'll keep him off the streets someday. Gotta set a little time aside for the boy, ya know? You gotta pitch to him, hit to him, teach him the game now while he's in his prime," he added.

My mother reminded me that my daughter also

needed more attention. "Kimberly is an artistic genius. Just look at this drawing," she said, holding a piece of paper with a finger painting of what looked like a dark-haired chicken with hemorrhoids, that had GRANDMA scrawled across the top.

"This talent cannot be wasted. Sophie Tannenbaum's granddaughter goes to special art classes after school. Such a shame you can't find the time to take our girl."

Then, from Father O'Connor: "Missed the children at religious services last week, Mrs. Krause. Must keep up with their spiritual training."

I did my best. Between baseball practice, art classes, Sunday school, cooking and cleaning, I managed to work, but did little else.

My friends worried. "I know this great-looking fireman who is single and looking," my friend Ellie said one day.

"Great idea," I answered, "ask him if he'll be free in ten years. My Saturday nights belong to Little League until then."

Just about the time I was thinking that single motherhood and sanity were not compatible, and that I should tell Ellie to call the fireman, a call came in to clean a house in nearby Warwick.

On a sunny afternoon three weeks earlier, a single mother, working as a junior bank executive, and her two small daughters, were killed inside their home. The perpetrator was not a leering, jeering madman, but their 15-year-old neighbor.

Twenty-eight days later, I cleaned that home. I picked up teddy bears and dolls from the bedroom floor and wiped down the kitchen. On a counter near the refrigerator was their mother's appointment book. I flipped the pages— it was crammed with business commitments.

I scrubbed all day...until every trace of life was removed.

That evening I cooked a big meal, took the kids to a movie and started thinking about hiring a cleaning helper so I could cut back on my schedule.

It was also the night I quit complaining about being a single mom.

"Opportunity is missed by most people because it comes dressed in overalls and looks like work."

–THOMAS EDISON

Motivated by my strained back and sorely-stretched soul, I decided, during the third year, to hire a friend to help me clean.

The good news about being a dependable cleaning lady is that it ensures customer loyalty. It is also the bad news. None of my customers wanted a stranger in their home. They had forgotten that three short years ago, in desperation, they had practically kidnapped me (a total stranger), entrusting me with getting their homes (and sometimes their lives) in order.

Since change is the enemy of complacency, I understood their reluctance to fix what they didn't think was broke. I also understood that if I didn't get a rest, I would be broken. One day I'd just disintegrate into a million pieces, get sucked up like so many dust mites in a vacuum cleaner bag, thrown away, never to be seen again.

I had to do something!

Finally, I mailed a letter to all my clients informing them that I was taking off the entire month of August. I was going to hang out with my kids, and recharge my physical and emotional batteries. The minute those letters were pulled from their mailboxes, ripped open and read, my phone went berserk. But my customers' frantic pleadings did not keep me from my commitment to rest and relaxation. It did, however, open the door of opportunity for my temporary replacement and—ultimately, for me.

Denise, a 28-year-old friend of mine, was eager to leave her hotel housekeeping job. Her daily cleaning quota there was 20 rooms. This translated into making 20 beds requiring 20 sets of linen, scouring 20 showers, and replacing 40 bottles of shampoo and moisturizer—to name just a few of the tasks she had to wade through each day. By contrast, cleaning three homes a day seemed like a walk in the park. So, it was settled. I provided her with a cleaning schedule, instructions, equipment, and a heartfelt pat on the back.

My previously reluctant customers warmed to her like butter on hot toast. She delighted them with tidy tricks like tri-fold towels, v-fold toilet tissue ends, and chocolate mints folded in foil wrappers which she lovingly left on their pillows. Out of habit, she even wanted to trash the used soaps and replace them with new. But eventually she got a grip.

August passed quickly. Feeling renewed and raring to go, I decided to team up with Denise so we could tackle each day's cleaning jobs together. The customers welcomed me back, filling me in on the gossip of their lives and raving about Denise. Everyone should have been content, right? Well, everyone was—except me.

Surprisingly, the role I thought I couldn't get away from fast enough, suddenly became a treasured possession. It's potential loss symbolized the loss of my identity. If I wasn't a cleaning lady, who the heck was I?

I dimly began to make out the word C-H-A-N-G-E flashing a warning in my brain. At the same time, the light of a higher purpose that had warmed me earlier came to life again. After all, the biggest career change I'd had to make in recent years had been adjusting to a one-month vacation.

I knew instinctively this wouldn't be the same kind of small change. It would be a B-I-G one that would alter my destiny forever. Far from welcoming this new opportunity, I mentally tried to shut the door on it. It looked like work, and I was overwhelmed with fear.

Few things in life are as difficult for us to digest, or as nourishing to our souls, as change. We cling tenaciously to the status quo, wallowing in its familiarity, suffocating ourselves as we try to cut the lifeline on anything that even remotely smacks of change. It was time for me to stop, reassess, realign. Fearful and confused, but with a glimmer of trust, I tentatively stepped back and watched while my life shot dramatically forward.

Denise continued cleaning for most of these clients, all of whom had friends and family on a waiting list. They began calling, and Denise and I agreed on how we would split the money. Soon I hired a second helper. Then a third. When the sixth employee came on board, I moved the equipment and supplies out of my garage and into a small, rented office.

I visited our customers occasionally and often spoke to them by phone. The gals filled me in on the latest happenings each afternoon when they came back to the shop to stash their supplies. For a while I even continued cleaning for a few of my original customers, and I was the one who filled in when one of the gals was sick.

So it was that I let go of the role that had become so familiar to me. I had "lost" my old identity, but so much more was gained. My circle of friends widened, and we all ministered to one another in many new and empowering ways.

2

Cleaning Up Dirty Messes

Most of my customers were appreciative and honest. Once in a while, however, someone would challenge my better nature. Mrs. Lareau taught me that not everyone will treat me fairly. Also, I learned that what someone else thinks about me doesn't matter; what matters is what I think about myself.

We stand behind our cleaning jobs. Our letterhead said, "Your complete satisfaction guaranteed. We want to know if we've missed a spot."

And over the years we did. Some spots were as tiny as a cat hair on a rug. Goofs included rooms that were missed, forgotten or not cleaned well enough.

We offered a service, an intangible product that could not be held, smelled or tasted. Its only value was in the eyes of our customers. And sometimes customers saw things differently. Take Mrs. Lareau, a 50ish dog trainer who had purchased a 60-year-old house vacated five years earlier.

"How much would it cost to make it sparkle?" she

wanted to know. We discussed how many rooms, how much dirt and settled on a price.

Becky, Tammy and Linda showed up at 8 a.m. and met Mrs. Lareau, accompanied by her growling Rottweiler, Buffy. "She's an orphan dog I'm training," she told the skeptical crew.

The house, a three-story wooden dowager, must have been abandoned for decades: ancient wallpaper was smeared with oily finger prints and scuff marks. Dirt and plate-sized water spots had stained the termite-eaten oak floors.

Cobwebs swung from corners, and antique windows were brown with stains. The bathrooms and kitchen were covered in a layer of grease that had attracted dust, creating a brown sludge. In one bedroom a litter box held what appeared to be calcified mold.

"It's been neglected just a tad," Mrs. Lareau observed breezily to the gals. "But you all can put the sparkle back into it."

"A tad?" asked Becky, the most outspoken of the group. "You call this a tad? Uh, Mrs. Lareau, I don't mean to be impolite, but, I don't think this place could ever be brought back up to sparkle quality. We can ungrease it, uncobweb it, uncrayon the walls and unscum the bathrooms, but sparkle is out of the question."

"Oh, I see," she said, hesitantly. "Well then, just do the best you can."

And, for the next two days Becky, Tammy and Linda did just that. Up and down ladders, on dirty floors and over brooms they strained, stretched and creaked, reeking of filth at the end of each day. They even cleaned Buffy's droppings silently, not wishing to confront their customer with evidence she had failed with her own canine client.

The gals worked from eight to three, scarfing their lunch in their cars. Mrs. Lareau stayed with them the entire time, yanking Buffy on a leash when his growls intensified. With each completed room she gushed, "Oh, what a difference."

Everyone except Buffy appeared delighted and appreciative—until it was time to pay.

Our policy was: we work, you pay, same day. We told customers this was necessary because we were a small outfit and needed to keep paperwork to a minimum. The truth is that customers stiffed us occasionally and we needed the money to meet our payroll.

We let Mrs. Lareau slide on her bill, which totaled over $500, until the end of the cleaning job, because she had stayed with the gals the entire time they were cleaning and seemed so appreciative.

At the end of the second day, Becky asked for the check. "Oh," said Mrs. Lareau, acting surprised, "I completely forgot and left my checkbook at the other house."

Becky, who knew an omen when one floated by, called the office. "Possible Code: Deadbeat here," she said.

Mrs. Lareau came to the phone, and I started the spiel.

"How did the job go?" I asked per our usual strategy. Commit them to customer satisfaction first, create perceived value for our services, then ask for the check.

"Oh," she bubbled, "it looks like a new house."

We chatted for a few minutes. Just as the movers were coming, we bonded, customer to cleaning boss. When I thought we had established a comfortable rapport, I reviewed our payment policy and suggested we would wait right there while she dashed off to the other house, grabbed her checkbook and returned to settle the account.

"Oh, no," she answered, "the girls are so tired. I am sure they are anxious to get home to their families. I will just stick the check in the mail tonight and save everyone the bother."

She certainly saved herself the bother. A week later, the check had still not arrived. I called her. Then I called her again, leaving twelve messages.

Two weeks later, a certified letter arrived. Becky read it to us. Mrs. Lareau explained she did not intend to pay a single dime for the job because we had done shoddy work and damaged her home. My workers had been lazy and we shouldn't be in business. If we pursued the matter and harassed her, the letter said, she would sue us for damage done to her home. Our dog trainer had become a cunning dragon lady.

"Lousy job?" Linda asked incredulously.

"Damage!" added Becky. "The only damage done in that place was to our backs."

"A misunderstanding?" I wondered.

"Definitely," Becky snapped. "This woman doesn't understand paying for services rendered. My guess is that she never intended to pay for this cleaning in the first place. This letter is her slippery way out."

Tammy, who had been listening quietly, looked up and said, "Why don't we just take her to Small Claims Court?"

Did we want to throw Mrs. Lareau in the slammer? I wondered. This was new. In the past we had used threats, dunning letters, and several times, police intervention for small bounced checks. But never a lawsuit. I didn't have to be an attorney to know that we had been had. I picked up her letter and read it myself.

A distant memory flashed through my mind. One afternoon, five years before, I had picked up my daughter, Kim, from school. As she ran into the car, tears streamed down her face. In a cracked voice, she explained how several of her second-grade girlfriends had tormented her at recess with the following rhyme:

> *Kimmy's mom just cleans all day,*
> *She's dirty, yucky, poo.*
> *My mommy said she's not too smart,*
> *And very stinky too!*

I thought about that time, when I was a newly single mother with two babies to feed, struggling with the decision to accept welfare or go to work. It was clear to me then, as it was now, that the only way I could possibly retain the few shreds of dignity I had left, was to make my way in this world with independence, grit and fortitude. Although, at the time, my options were limited to house-cleaning, I was determined to do it with honor and be the best darn cleaning lady possible. I realized not everyone would see housekeeping as a dignified profession, and that the only person who had to see it that way was me.

I had gathered Kim up in my arms, wiped her tears away and said, "What matters most in this world is the dignity and honor we find in our hearts. In God's economy, nothing is wasted. And in His eyes, we are all magnificent and worthy. When it comes time for you to choose a path, never let anyone put you down or take advantage of you. Always hold your head up high. If you do, you will realize that someone else's cruel words or unfairness have nothing to do with who you really are. It just shows how poor that person is inside."

"Let's do it," I said to everyone, slapping palms, wondering if I would confront Mrs. Darth Vader herself in that courtroom. We wrote Mrs. Lareau a letter outlining our intentions and offering a last chance to pay up before the Law's long arm swooped down, plucked her from her dust-free bedroom, and dropped her into an eight-by-eight cement cell.

A few days later, she left a phone message that we would never see a nickel of her money. Buffy was growling in the background. Becky figured out that she owed us about 10,000 nickels altogether, so the next day I went to the courthouse to file paperwork charging Mrs. Margaret Lareau with being a delinquent consumer.

"What's the charge?" a young woman asked.

"Being a fugitive from payment," I answered, trying to sound lawyerly.

"Beg your pardon?" she said, snapping her gum.

"She stiffed us," I explained.

"Okay," she said, filling in the blanks on the form, "sign here."

I signed there and there and there, handed over ten bucks and asked her what came next. She popped another bubble, reached under the counter and pulled out a 125-page "booklet" of "easy to follow" Small Claims Court procedures.

Back in the office, we read through the booklet and meticulously prepared our case. We rehearsed and role-played. At one point Tammy took on the role of Mrs. Lareau, talking about how she wasn't going to pay, and Becky played herself, saying how she should. They started yelling at each other: our preparation for "People's Court" was deteriorating.

On court day, I arrived at Justice's doors with a manila folder stuffed with worksheets, Mrs. Lareau's nasty letter, and written testimony from the gals about their work. Wrapped in a plastic bag were some of the reeking rags used to clean one of Mrs. Lareau's bathrooms. I was as prepared as I could be. As we were called to the bench, I looked at Mrs. Lareau, thought of the gals, and started to fume.

"What's that smell?" the judge asked, sniffing the air as we approached the bench.

"Dirty rags, your honor," I said, pulling a few out of the plastic bag and handing them to the sheriff, who walked them over to the judge. "I would like to have them admitted as Exhibit Number One," I added.

The judge was a tall, bald black man who looked more like basketball star Shaquille O'Neal than People's Court star Judge Wapner. With an outstretched arm and two fingers, he picked up one corner of a yellowed rag, dangling it as far away from his body as his reach would permit.

"Exhibit Number One?" he asked.

"Yes, sir," I answered and pulled out Exhibit Number Two, the vacuum cleaner bag used to contain Mrs. Lareau's dirt. I handed it over to the clerk, who plopped it down in front of the judge. Dust and hair balls puffed out of the hole in the paper bag and the judge sneezed several times.

"Wha-a-the heck?" he stammered.

"Forensic evidence, your honor," I explained.

"Forensic evidence?" He started to howl. "Ms. Krause," he exclaimed through the dusty fog, "this is *not* a murder case!"

I felt like a five-year-old. I looked down for a moment, shifting from one foot to the other.

"This is Small Claims Court. In this courtroom we listen to *civil* cases. We attempt to resolve minor disputes in a *civil* manner, rather than *killing* each other!"

He coughed, then sneezed again.

"So, Ms. Krause, unless you plan on murdering the defendant in the near future, this forensic evidence is not relevant and cannot be part of your testimony. Is this clear?"

I nodded my head. From the corner of my eye, I could see Mrs. Lareau smiling triumphantly.

"Are you absolutely sure?" he asked impatiently, handing down the evidence to the clerk, then wiping his hands on his robe.

I nodded again.

"Fine," he said, pounding the gavel. "The court will take a twenty minute recess and I suggest, Ms. Krause, that during those twenty minutes, you prepare to state your side of this case as clearly and simply as possible, minus the forensic evidence." Then he got down from the bench and went into his chambers, blowing his nose on the way.

I scowled at Mrs. Lareau. Her face had broken into a broad grin. I considered murdering her and resubmitting the evidence.

When the judge returned, he sat patiently as I nervously began to tell what really happened.

"Were you there during the cleaning?" he asked.

Heat crept up the back of my neck. I saw where this line of questioning was headed. I stalled for time to prepare a defense. I asked him to repeat the question. I heard someone from Mrs. Lareau's direction cough.

"No, your honor," I finally answered, "I was not there."

"Well then," he continued, "how can you testify to the quality of work that was performed?"

I couldn't.

Mrs. Lareau snickered as I sat down.

How could everything get so turned around? What about the dirty rags? And vacuum cleaner bag? And written testimony? Why was I being interrogated anyway? This wasn't anything like the People's Court, where the good guys usually won.

The judge turned to the defendant, now on the stand. She sobbed about the injustices our company had inflicted on her, complained about being overcharged and about our shoddy work. Then she handed over her own evidence: "before and after" cleaning pictures of her worn tub and faded bathroom wallpaper. "They ruined my home," she sniffled.

The judge studied the photos for a long time, looked

down at the dirty rags and vacuum cleaner bag sitting at the clerk's feet, at Mrs. Lareau, and at me.

Then he sat back, folded his long arms, closed his eyes and processed the facts. Finally, he leaned forward, tucked his hands under his chin and asked Mrs. Lareau in a quiet voice about the approximate age of her home.

"Sixty years old," she said.

"Is this the original bathroom wallpaper?" he asked, holding up the photo.

"Yes, sir."

"And, Mrs. Lareau," he continued, "am I correct that you are not disputing the fact that three cleaning people were at your home on two separate days for seven hours each day?"

She shuffled her feet. "No, sir."

"I see. On these two separate occasions, Mrs. Lareau," he went on, "did they sit around watching TV, or did they clean your home to the best of their ability?"

She shifted her eyes to the floor, "They cleaned."

"Let me see if I have this straight," he said. "You hired three cleaning personnel and agreed ahead of time on an hourly rate. Then they showed up at your home and did the work they were hired for to the best of their ability? Is that correct?"

She stammered, "Yes, but..."

"Mrs. Lareau," the judge said, looking her directly in the eye, "are you aware that slavery has been abolished in this country? People are paid for work they do these days."

She winced.

"Here is what I am going to do. Since you seem to be a reasonable lady, I will give you an opportunity to pay the amount owed today, right here, before this court."

He leaned forward. "Or you may choose not to pay. This is a democratic society and it is your decision. If that is the case, I will at that point be forced to issue a judgment against you. That judgment will be followed forty-eight hours later by a body attachment. This attachment is then given to a sheriff, who will come to your home, place you in his car and drive you to the county jail where you will be retained until your obligation is met."

She whipped out her checkbook and pen and began scribbling furiously.

I struggled not to grin.

We had won our case in court, as well as the case for standing up for ourselves, no matter what anyone else thought.

"And Ms. Krause," the judge said turning to me, "please be sure to pick up your forensic evidence from the clerk on the way out." I started to walk toward the clerk. "One more thing," he stated from the bench. I stopped and turned around.

"I would also like to suggest," he smiled, "that you cut back a little on the Perry Mason reruns."

3

When Your Dreams Turn to Dust..Vacuum

One day someone publicly acknowledged my acting talents in a national magazine — the talents I had given up on long ago to become a mom and business owner. Although I was content in my life, after reading that article, I suddenly had regrets about missing the "Hollywood" boat. I was reunited with the man who made those comments several years later and realized my star was burning brightly right where I was.

A long time ago I was a stage star with high self-esteem. When I was seventeen, and in high school, I auditioned for a high school play by Lillian Hellman entitled, *The Little Foxes*. The play is about a Southern family trying to deal with problem relatives. There was drunken Aunt Birdie, the part I played, and her husband, Oscar, a brute who battered Birdie around a bunch, played by a skinny kid named James Woods.

Jimmy and I grew up on opposite sides of town, but his mother, Martha, knew my aunt Delores, who found it quaint that we kids were playing a drunk and a wife batterer.

I got into acting because I didn't like myself and my guess is that Jimmy's motivation was the same. When we were up there on that stage being someone else, our self-esteem shot way up off the charts. It was magic! We came alive by hiding inside a character. We could say anything, do anything, be anyone. Together, we were something else!

Miss Donahue, our director, said we were like Tracy and Hepburn. The State judges said we were the best actors they had ever seen and gave us arms full of awards.

A couple of years later, after an education at Cambridge, Jimmy headed to the Big Apple's bright lights to become a movie star. I headed west to Las Vegas's bright lights to become a teenage bride.

I followed Jimmy's career over the years, whether I wanted to or not, because when I moved back to Rhode Island, his brother's video store was one block from my cleaning shop. I'd rent tapes from Michael and he always filled me in on the latest Jimmy trivia. When he told me that Jimmy's asking price was up to $5 million a movie, I promptly raised my cleaning rates. After all, I figured, everything's relative.

I thought I was doing well with my cleaning business until a winter day in 1987 when Jimmy's mother, Martha, called my Aunt Delores, who called my father, Diego, who was outside in his garden at the time. Aunt Delores told my father to hurry out and buy a copy of *Cosmopolitan* magazine. Now, my father is a house painter who plants tomatoes in the back yard. He had never heard of *Cosmopolitan* magazine. He asked my mother, "What is this thing?"

My mother explained it to him. "It has movie stars in it with no clothes on and they cover it up in the super-market with brown paper."

"Delores said to buy one," he explained to my mother.

"I don't care what Delores says," my mother yelled, picking up the wooden gravy spoon and pointing it at him. "You are not bringing one of those things into this house!"

Well, they finally brought it into the house because Aunt Margaret, who bought the *National Enquirer* every week and knew a lot about movie star stuff, told my mother that the naked women were all in another magazine.

After they read the story, they drove over to my cleaning shop and left the whole magazine in my mailbox, with a note on the door that said, "Your mother and I were here." (I probably would have guessed that because two smooshy tomato seeds were still stuck to the upper right hand corner of the note. My father obviously was in a hurry to bring it over.)

A short while later, I returned and took the magazine out of the mailbox. I flipped through to page 114. There was Jimmy Wood's tribute to...me.

> *"He was also enthralled by the work of a 17-year-old tough Italian-looking girl named Joyce Curci, who played Birdie to his Oscar. She was just a high school kid like him, but he was dazzled by her performance. 'She was one of the greatest natural actresses I've seen in my life. And I've seen them all. I've worked*

with most of them. But there was never a moment in the theater that was as powerful as that. I truly believed. I wanted to be like that.'"

I closed up shop and began to drive home. About a block from the video store, I pulled over and started to cry. I cried because I was sitting in a 10-year-old Dodge Omni with a muffler that was taped to the tail pipe and two five-year-old retreads with the steel poking through. I cried because I was driving home to a messy house because I was so busy cleaning other homes I had no time to clean my own.

I cried because Jimmy probably never worried about stuff like that. He probably had a new limousine every year and a chauffeur named Charles and a butler named Cheeves and a poodle named Chi Chi and a personal dog groomer named Candy.

And I cried mostly because, for all those years, he got to hide behind a bunch of characters and feel good about himself, while I had to be out front, off-stage, and feeling crummy about myself.

And I stayed feeling crummy and thinking that Jimmy had it made. Then I saw him at his step-father's wake in our hometown some time later. There he was, standing in the receiving line, smiling at me, hugging me, telling me that I hadn't changed a bit, lying to me Hollywood-style and leading me, arm around my shoulder, to the seats in the back of the room "where we could be quiet, just the two of us, and catch up on old times."

Tracy and Hepburn, all over again, we thought, reuniting, revisiting, reliving Birdie and Oscar and being seventeen again. Just us, the movie star and the cleaning lady, reshooting the breeze that blew by twenty-five years ago. Except he was doing all the talking and I was doing all the listening. "Hey, do you remember...?" "Yeah, did you see the look on Miss Donahue's face?" "Whadid you think when that drama judge...?"

Suddenly it hit me. This guy makes millions of dollars on every picture. Of course he's doing all the talking. I wondered how many floors I would have to scrub for a fraction of that, and I got angry.

"Drama coach? What do you care about a drama coach we had twenty-five years ago when you played my husband, Oscar? I mean, your brother told me that you were nominated for a *real* Oscar this year. And another thing, what could you possibly care about my life or where I've been or who I've seen? You, the big movie star. The five-million-dollar man." And I sat up straight and crossed my arms and stuck my chin out in a defiant way, just waiting, just waiting for him to try another one of his buddy-buddy ploys on me.

He took his arm away from my shoulder and dropped his eyes for what seemed like a long, long time. When they looked back up into mine, they were wet with real Jimmy tears. There was no Hollywood in those tears, no "Hey howaya, Babe," no "Look at me, Mr. Bright Lights." It was just my old high school chum, Jimmy. He was back and we were sitting here in our old hometown and we were friends.

"Let me tell you about Hollywood," he began. And for the next 20 minutes, I sat on a fold-out wooden chair, in the back of the funeral parlor, listening to James

Woods tell me about his struggle up the ladder, the heartaches, the constant battle to stay on top, the lack of privacy, and how quickly today's winners could become tomorrow's losers.

And I listened real close when he said to me, just before he got up and walked wearily back in line, "Do you have any idea how lucky you are to have two healthy children? To be able to walk down the street quietly? To have friends who like you simply for who you are? To be your own boss?" Then, getting up to leave, he said, "At least you still have your self."

Suddenly, he was gone, and I never got a chance to thank him for the important gift he gave me that day.

So, Jimmy, if you're listening, thank you for exposing me to a new role. Since the last time I saw you, I've been playing the part of Joy Krause (a.k.a. Joyce Curci)... Contented Woman.

4

Understanding the Labels

Through her example, Barbara D'Angellino taught me about unconditional love. I always try to see something good in the people around me and to tell them what I see.

She walked in on a blizzardy January morning, ten minutes early for her appointment, wearing a green wool skirt, a matching silk ruffled blouse and penny loafers each with a shiny penny in its coin slot. Her hair was gathered into a little ponytail in back and tied up neat as could be with a silky green ribbon. She was looking for a job.

After a busy Christmas season at the cleaning shop, I decided to expand our services and become more professional. My business plan was written by gut instinct and implemented on an "as needed" basis, usually with crossed fingers. Future goals were scientifically analyzed during weekly pow-wows, which were fueled by chocolate-chip cookies and Coca Cola. Suggestions were bandied about, bounced around and, if they landed right-side up, we tested 'em. Our Research and Development Department was always on the lookout for innovations in quality and training.

We would pull straws to see who would interview new applicants. Sandy got into it so much she gave them pop quizzes after making them watch a cleaning video we had made. "Quick! Which size refill bag does the Panasonic #211 take?" or, "At the count of three, tell me which cleaner do you use first for heavy-duty soap scum in the shower?"

Some women couldn't handle the quiz and left immediately. Others got some of the answers right. The woman with the penny loafers, Barbara D'Angellino, got a perfect score.

After Sandy quizzed her about the video, Barbara filled out her application at a nearby desk, peering down through round, rimless granny glasses. Beside the line that said, "Education: College," she wrote in, "See attached."

The "attached" was six paragraphs listing the colleges and universities Barbara had attended during her educated life. Next to each were all the seminars and classes she had taken in those institutions. Then came her special awards, her degrees and finally, the initials she collected along the way: BA and MFA and Ph.D.

After an hour and a half of writing, she put the application down on the desk and thanked us all for our time. We said we would let her know, and she left.

"What happens if she breaks a nail?" asked Denise, who had dropped out of junior college in her second year.

It turned out that Barbara D'Angellino, who came to work with us the very next day, broke a lot of nails over the next year. She also broke, as we would later learn, a few misconceptions about people who have letters after their names.

Denise, the most cynical, offered to bet on how long Barbara would last. We told her Barbara seemed eager to clean and was not at all pompous. Besides, I told Denise, we had to give her a chance. We hadn't seen a perfect score on our video before. Denise said she would give us odds.

Denise would have lost the bet because Barbara showed up every day. In fact, she showed up early each morning, eager to work with all our clients, even taciturn Mr. Oglesby. She would fill her spray bottles with liquid cleaners, pick up the scouring cleanser, grab some rags and a vacuum and head out to the clients' homes.

Around 2 p.m. she would stroll in, carefully put away the bottles and rags, rinse her hands and turn down our offers of a slab of pizza. When leaving, she would always take the time to say, "Have a nice afternoon."

After about a month, Denise couldn't take Barbara's formal friendliness and optimism any more. After a few of these good-natured goodbyes from Barbara, one day Denise waved and yelled, "I think you're a weirdo," to see if she could get a reaction.

"See you all bright and early," Barbara responded, adding "I'm sorry you had an arduous day, Denise."

"An arduous day? Know what I think?" Denise

shot back, unimpressed as the door closed. "I think she's a spy."

"Yeah, we're really top secret," said Sandy. "Why doesn't she just steal our video? We could call it *The Secrets of Mr. Clean.* You know, Denise, you're the one with the problem. Leave her alone."

"We are only a cleaning company, not a uranium factory," I reminded Denise, who was pacing the floor.

"Maybe she's on the lam. All I know is something is weird about this girl," Denise insisted. "First of all, she is *too* happy. And second of all, she is too smart. No offense, but do you think I would work here if I had a Ph.D.? And third of all, why does she carry that beeper and notepad around in her pocket?"

She had me on the third one because I wondered the same thing myself. Denise had noticed the bulge in Barbara's shirt pocket one day as Barbara was pouring heavy-duty cleaner into her spray bottles.

"Ah, ha," said Denise when Barbara left, "we're being taped."

I told Denise she was being paranoid. "Who would buy a tape of people filling up bottles?" I asked.

"Mark my words," she said, "that girl is up to something. I don't know about you, but I plan to keep a real close eye on her."

And she did. All winter, then all spring and summer. She even tried to grill Barbara in a subtle way, questioning her about her weekend on Mondays, and on Fridays about any parties she planned to attend. Barbara's response was consistent. She spent all her time with her family, she would say, offering nothing more.

"Find anything subversive yet?" I teased Denise on

a slow June day. "Microphones hidden under the rags? Cameras stashed behind the air-conditioning ducts?"

"Very funny," said Denise, smirking. "You wait."

The explanation finally came, in the form of Mrs. Anameiter, a client in her 80's. Our arrangement had been to spend two hours cleaning her home every Tuesday. But what Mrs. Anameiter had really wanted for two hours a week was someone to talk to. She had gotten Barbara.

"Look at this," said Denise, waving a note in my face. It arrived in the morning mail. The note said:

Barbara, dear,

> *I was just sitting here thinking about you and hoping things worked out this week with your brother. Please do not worry about getting beeped and having to rush off. We will catch up next time.*
> *You are a very courageous young lady. Keep up the good work...and the writing!*

> *Your friend,*
> *Mrs. Annabelle Anameiter*

"See that! She gets beeped! She's using us for a cover. Now who is paranoid?" Denise wanted to know, waving her arms around for effect.

On our machine was a message from Barbara. "Hi, everybody. It's Barbara. Sorry to have to tell you this, but I will need some time off. I need to take care of something at home. Have a nice day."

Hot on Barbara's trail, Denise offered to take Mrs. Anameiter's cleaning slot.

"I wondered who they would send," Mrs. Anameiter said when she opened the door to Denise.

"You knew she was skipping town?" asked Denise, leaning on a broom.

"Lovely girl, that Barbara," said Mrs. Anameiter, inviting Denise in. "So brave for her age. Seems unfair that she is the only family left to care for Scotty. It can't be easy working all day, worrying if her beeper will go off, and if she will need to rush home. Some tea first, dear?"

For the next two hours Denise sat at Mrs. Anameiter's kitchen table and listened to the story of Barbara, Scotty and the beeper.

Denise learned about the accident six months earlier in which Barbara's mother and father were killed—the one that paralyzed her 19-year-old brother Scott.

She heard about Barbara quitting her senior editor's job with Random House in New York City, the one she had spent eight years working up to.

She learned about the doctor's warning that Scott needed to be institutionalized because he couldn't care for himself. And that Barbara refused to put him in one of those places, which meant she had to give up her career and find work near her parents' home. Something not too demanding, with no nights or weekends. A job she could leave during the day if she had to and something that would get them by for the time being.

"She still writes, you know. Poems and short stories.

Used to bring me one every week. Did you know she does that for all her customers? Wonderful girl, that Barbara."

Denise was quiet when she came back to the shop.

"I was wrong," she said in a quiet voice to Sandy and me, who had gotten up to hear the dirt on our fugitive hire.

Denise sat alone for half an hour in the back room. When I found her, she had located a pad of yellow-lined paper and written the following letter:

Dear Barbara,

> *I do not have much education and no fancy initials after my name like you. But I always thought I was pretty smart about life and people. Today, as I sit here writing you this letter, I am not so sure.*

> *What I am sure of is that I am much smarter because of you. Here is what you have taught me.*

> *You taught me about love. Deep, unconditional love from one human being to another.*

> *You taught me about unselfishness and sometimes putting the needs of others before my own without moaning and groaning about it.*

> *You taught me about the unfairness of judging others before I get to know them and what their lives are like.*

> *You taught me about pride and finding honor in everything I do, no matter how humble the task.*

> *You taught me that fancy titles and fancy initials weren't important. I learned the only initials*

that count are D or F or H or L because they
stand for Decency and Faith and Humility and Love.
*   And, last but not least, you taught me that even*
really smart people can break fingernails and
deal with it.

Thanks for the education,

Your friend,

Denise

Six months later, Denise signed up for a writing class at the junior college...with Barbara as her mentor and editor.

5

Pick Yourself Up, Dust Yourself Off and Start All Over Again

Middle age is like underwear—it just keeps creeping up on you. One day I was 27, then when I looked up again I was 45. What's weird about growing older is that it happens so fast, we seldom have a chance to adjust to the change. So, imagine my surprise when my son started to point out some things I'd been doing all my life that I probably shouldn't be doing now because of "my age."

I disagreed. I think we can be young forever, if we choose, and keep having a blast while we last. How old am I? In some ways, I'm not even born yet. And in other ways, I'm a teenager and I'm struggling and I'm rebelling. And in other ways, I'm ancient; I'm 2,000 years old. A trip to the mountains helped my son, Mark, and me realize that age is simply a number.

Franklin D. Roosevelt said, "The only thing we have to fear, is fear itself." He may have pulled a war-weary nation together with those words, but I know he never climbed a mountain. Which is what I did recently to prove a point.

All because of my 19-year-old son.

Mark, who spent his childhood around wet suits and wind surfers, had traded his lobster pots in for snow tires and Timberland boots when he moved to Colorado his freshman college year.

My son's move to the mountains was typical of his childhood. He was a dreamer, a risk taker—qualities, he said, he must have gotten from his father. His mother, apparently, was boringly old and sedentary.

One day he asked me if people my age still had sex.

"Things pretty much dry up and fall off at 50," I said matter-of-factly. He thought about that for a while and about the 31 years he had left. Within minutes, he invited his glamorous girlfriend over for pizza and videos.

He thought I should act my age, give up henna rinses and let my hair go natural. "Mom, face it," he reminded me one day, "you are getting old."

He also thought that people as old as I am should not wear Guess? jeans or Reeboks. Or go to rock concerts. Or roll around in the grass with the dog. Or ski the back trails. Or go mountain climbing because he thought we were all, at this stage of life, over the hill.

So, he was surprised when I called him at school and said, "Mark, I want to come out for a visit and climb one of those hills you think I have already crossed over."

"Mom...these aren't hills," he said patiently. "They are mountains. Cold and dangerous mountains. I couldn't be responsible for you."

"No problem," I answered, unwilling to back down,

"what will I need to bring?"

"Mom," he tried to reason, "you know there are bears out here, right?"

Bears? I had not considered bears. It was November. Shouldn't they be snoring in their caves by now?

No backing down, I thought. Either I struck a blow for the women and mothers of the world or I would remain a yellow-bellied, dried-up, polyester, cellulite pool of antique weenieism, terrified of heights and petrified of any animal larger than a poodle.

I knew this moment was a rite of passage for my son and me. Could I prove that varicose veins and crow's feet were just clever disguises for the wild child within? Or were they?

"No sweat," I said, walking with the phone over to the freezer door to reach for Ben and Jerry's Chunky Monkey, the only wild animal I could face at the moment.

"Okay," he answered with a shrug. "Then bring along some hiking boots, long underwear, wool gloves, thermal socks, knit hat, ear muffs, a down-filled coat, a few turtlenecks and ski pants."

"Will I need my hot rollers?" I asked.

"Only if you think it'll make a difference to a grizzly bear," he said. I found the stuff he recommended at an Army Surplus store, raced home and packed everything, along with Alka-Seltzer and my hot rollers (you never know what other wild thing you might meet on a mountain) and hopped an evening flight.

Mark met me at the airport at 8 a.m. wearing a broad Stetson.

"What happened to your Red Sox hat?" I asked.

He looked around quickly to see if anybody had heard me. "Mom," he whispered, "this is Colorado. You can't mention the Red Sox."

I wondered what else I couldn't mention as we hopped into his Nissan Pathfinder and headed out. "Can I talk now?" I asked.

"Okay," he said, closing the door, "we're alone."

"What's that music you're playing?"

"Waylon Jennings."

"Who?"

My son, who just six months ago revered Jethro Tull and Pink Floyd, retorted, "You don't know who Waylon Jennings is?" I was beginning to wonder if I was in the right country and if this was my son. "He's just about the hottest country singer there is, along with Johnnie Cash and Willie Nelson. Everybody around here plays their music. They're legends who were all into drugs once," he informed me knowingly.

"Mark," I asked, hesitantly, "you like it around here?"

"Sure, Mom," he answered, "it's wild." I felt faint.

We cruised north along Route 25, heading toward the mountains—the Rhode Island cowboy and his wide-eyed mom, bouncing up and down in a truck.

"What are those things?" I asked, pointing to some strange-looking creatures in a meadow off the highway.

"Buffalo."

"Like on a nickel? Like on the plains? Like in bison?"

"Mom," my son said, getting exasperated, "this is the West. They have animals like that out here."

"Of course," I said, looking out the window.

"Now, when we get to where we're going," he

informed me, "I might have to stop the truck fast, so make sure your seatbelt is on tight."

I tightened the belt and looked at him. "Mind telling me why?" I asked, not really wanting to know.

"Elk," he said. "All over the place. Coyotes, too." I shut my eyes and grabbed the door handle.

He stopped the truck in a place called Estes Park and pulled up to a cabin cluster called "Mountain Man Cabins." The sign said, "cable, kitchen, kozy and kleen." He went in to sign us up for the night. I looked around for bears.

"Last one on the end," Mark said, walking back to the truck and pointing to our mountain retreat. It looked like a Daniel Boone reject, lopsided and breezy, something the big bad wolf could easily sneeze down.

"The lady in the office said to be careful not to trip over the gopher holes," my son said, clearly uncomfortable with the idea of camping with his mom.

Buffalo, elk, coyote, wolf and now...gophers. I wondered if we had made a wrong turn somewhere and ended up inside the San Diego Zoo.

"Better hurry up and change," he said. "Gotta get to the other side of that mountain before the sun starts to go down or we'll never make it back up. Wouldn't want to get stranded out there in the Rockies. Nasty way to go," he said, grinning.

I slipped the Alka-Seltzer into my coat pocket, unpacked my Samsonite and struggled into what seemed like all the clothes inside. I shuffled out of the cabin, padded arms out to the sides, quilted legs stiff, gasping for air the turtlenecks were shutting off.

"I'm ready," I croaked.

"Great," came the reply, "hop in." I didn't exactly hop. It was more like a roll, a stretch and a thump. "Harrrr-ump!" it went.

"We're off to the mountains! Yeeeee-ha!" he whooped, grinning and waving his cowboy hat out the window.

It was Waylon, Johnnie, Willie, Mark and me heading up Route 36 past the guard station that, by the way, was closed due to inclement weather, into God's country. I never realized God built his country so high. Every time we went around a corner, another road pointed straight up.

The road consisted of what I would jokingly call two lanes, obviously built when Volkswagens were still in style. Each sharp curve was framed on the outside by thin wooden fencing and, on the inside—the driving side—by a slice of protruding mountain, which made it impossible to see what was on the other side until we got there. The road tar looked white and slick.

"Mark, would that happen to be ice?" I wondered.

He shot me a glance that said, "Mom, this is Colorado. That's what they have around here." I silently recited the Lord's Prayer.

"Would you look at that view!" he yelled, pointing to the side.

"I'll look! I'll look! Just keep your eyes on the road!"

Below were vanilla snow cones dotted with green pine sprinkles. Elk roamed, deer drank from the lake below and strange-looking birds circled above.

He pulled the truck to the side of the road, somewhere midway to Heaven, and we got out, or rather, he got out. I rolled.

"Follow me," he said, stepping into snow that buried his boot immediately. I stepped in his footprint and stopped.

"Where are you going, son?" I asked, trying my best not to let him hear the panic in my voice.

He turned and looked at me proudly. "Mom," he said, "we are going to climb this mountain."

I looked up. Then I looked up again. "Mark," I asked quietly, "where is the top?"

"We'll know when we get there," he said, walking on.

If we get there, I thought, gritting my teeth and taking the first tentative step up. "That's one small step for this mom," I said silently. "One giant leap for motherhood. I am not afraid."

Then another. "I am doing this for everyone over forty. I am not afraid."

And another. "I am doing this because I have already started up this stupid mountain, and I'll be damned if I'll give up now."

I was losing breath. Breathe in courage, breathe out fear, I thought. But it was the noise, a crashing sound of branches as something came toward me, that nearly did me in. A huge buck ran across my path. I prepared to die, skewered on an antler. I knew Rudolph and this wasn't Rudolph. He looked at me and I thought I saw him grin before he turned and ran in another direction.

"Did you see that, Mom?" Mark yelled down.

"Beautiful," I sputtered, praying for energy to climb a few more steps. I wondered what happened to people who suffered heart attacks up here. Did they simply bury them nearby? I hoped if that occurred, Mark would realize that this had been my idea and he would not live out his life in guilt.

I kept on climbing. After what seemed like hours of walking in my son's footsteps, sniveling and sweating every inch of the way, we finally reached the top.

We sat and stared at the Colorado valley below, catching our breath. Mark looked over at me. I was drenched, shivering and happier than I could ever recall.

"Not bad," he said, smiling,"...for an old fart."

I tackled him and pushed his face in the snow. He got up and threw snowballs at me. I laughed until tears poured down my cheeks and crystallized.

We took pictures of each other covered in snow from head to foot. Then we rested the camera in the branch of a tiny pine tree and set it on auto-pilot. The camera took a picture of us both lying face to face in a snow drift, arm wrestling.

"Okay," he laughed, dropping his arm and winking at me, "I'll let you win this time Mrs.-Gray-Hair-Covered-Up-With-Henna."

I looked at my son. I looked at the mountain. I looked at me on top of that mountain. I turned to him and smiled.

"Sweetheart," I said, "many victories have been won with old, gray battleships leading the fleet."

6

Serving Leftovers Creatively

Becky and Mrs. Casey bonded during a state crisis. Barbara DeAngelis, in <u>Real Moments</u>, said, "Perhaps crisis forces us to return to our center when we have drifted away from our true values, and to put our lives in perspective when we have forgotten what is really important."

Mrs. Casey taught me to remember to share kindness in or out of a crisis.

By 1990, business was taking off. New customers called daily for help with spring cleaning, moving, parties and deaths. I hired twelve employees— a mix of single mothers, college students and displaced homemakers. In the summer we tied our hair into ponytails, and in shorts and T-shirts we scrubbed porches and spritzed patios. Winters found us in jeans, sweatshirts and boots, de-sludging sinks and washing floors. Most of the gals wore full makeup, earrings and other jewelry to their shifting job sites.

Teresa, who liked to credit Mr. Clean for funding her sophomore year in college, often said, "You never know when you might meet Mr. Right." What we lacked in sophistication, we made up for with enthusiasm.

Then disaster crashed down upon Rhode Island in the form of an economic boondoggle, making headlines in *Newsweek* and *The New York Times*, and closing down the state for two years. The problem began when a credit union owner fled the state with millions of his investors' dollars. The state decided to freeze the assets of other credit unions in order to avoid a rush on savings. Although the state opened the credit unions later, more than 300,000 Rhode Islanders discovered that their money had been placed in institutions which weren't federally insured.

"I feel like the census taker for death row," Teresa said one day between phone calls normally made to confirm the next day's appointments. Our longtime customer, Mr. Sinclair, had just told her that his company payroll was tied up and he was shutting down his operation. Another customer had shown up for work only to have an armed guard tell him that the company was closed indefinitely.

Everyone was sliding.

I knew we were in the same shape, and I had no answers for the gals. Becky was a single mom, recently remarried, who had worked her way off welfare when she joined my company. Nancy was using her salary for her son's college tuition. I wondered how large a salary cut I would have to take just to stay in business or if I could take a salary at all. Rhode Islanders were worrying about putting food on the table, not about who was going to wax it. We started cutting back. The van went first.

"How will we get around?" Denise asked.

"Like we used to," I said. "In our cars."

When the computer broke down, I put it in a box and stuck it in the closet, hoping no one saw my mouth quiver.

"How will we keep track of the schedules?" Peggy asked.

"Like we used to," I answered. "By hand."

They quit asking by the time we got around to canceling the payroll service and company gas cards.

"I know. I know," Denise said. "We're getting back to basics."

I was feeling hopeless. Then I learned the lesson from this crisis. It was taught to me, innocently enough, by Becky.

In the last six months she had become good friends with her client, Mrs. Casey. They had the kind of intimacy women share that springs from knowing where mops, toilet paper and the dirty laundry are stashed, the kind of closeness families share by knowing each others' special possessions and where they are hidden. After weeks of cleaning a counter-top, you learn to notice new touches—a new flower pot, the reorganization of a cupboard—little touches that an elderly widow like Mrs. Casey shared with no one else. That's the kind of bond we had with old timers.

Mrs. Casey was a wisp of a woman, shy and refined. She wore a short, gray bob pulled up on the sides with a barrette. Her hair was so thin you had to try not to be obvious by staring through it to her pink scalp. She was probably two generations older than Becky, who, with her chubby frame, curly red hair and freckles, would never be mistaken for Mrs. Casey's kin.

They were an unlikely couple. Becky never knew her own mother, who had abandoned her when she was six. The differences didn't end there. While Becky struggled to work, go to school and care for her first and fourth graders, Mrs. Casey had been left a very comfortable widow with the profits from Mr. Casey's haberdashery store. She could have afforded Becky more often than once every three weeks, but Mrs. Casey liked to keep her money "for a rainy day," as her husband had advised.

Unfortunately, she had kept it all in the now-defunct credit union. The rainy day had turned into a hurricane.

"I'm sorry, dear, but I'm going to be cleaning for myself from now on," Mrs. Casey told Becky one day on the phone. Becky said fine and hung up. The next morning she showed up at her usual time. She cleaned Mrs. Casey's home for months—no charge.

Some people in this world just seem to know when and how to do the right thing. The auto mechanic who dove into Seattle's frigid waters to save an airplane crash victim. Eighty-eight-year-old Osceola McCarthy, the Mississippi laundress who saved spare change all her life until she had enough to give a full scholarship to a young student. Heroes all, who soften the world with their kindness.

Here is how Becky explained her generosity, "I figured we were totally helpless over our customers' situation. But the one thing I *could* control was whether I could bring some happiness into that situation and into someone else's life." The volunteer effort ended before the credit union crisis was solved. One day Becky arrived an hour early and peered into the window when her knock went unanswered.

There sat Mrs. Casey, at the kitchen table, eating breakfast from a can of Friskie's dogfood.

When she finally opened the door, the two women held each other and cried.

Becky called Mrs. Casey's children in Boston, who drove right over and stocked her cabinets and checking account and immediately restored our cleaning contract.

We scraped through at the cleaning company for 18 months until the state unfroze people's money. One day, as we sipped coffee in our morning meeting, I suggested we reflect on what we learned and that we give thanks for the entire experience. Denise mooned me.

Rhode Islanders learned about the power of government, the vulnerability of banks and to hide their money under the mattress.

In our shop, we learned about streamlining operations and switching to generic-brand roasted coffee.

We also learned about loving others and selecting dog food: Pedigree Choice Cuts in Sauce With Chicken is a little bland, but Friskie's Gourmet Cuts in Gravy, heated up and sprinkled with parsley, is outstanding!

7

Picking Pine Needles Out of the Carpet

When the children were teenagers, I remarried and learned that people of all religions are more alike than not.

Once I tried being Jewish. At the same time, I tried being married for the second time. The results for both were similar: they worked—for a while.

With each decision, I consulted my family.

"Can I put meatballs instead of matzo balls in the soup?" my mother wondered.

My brother, an Italian tenor, asked, "Is it okay to sing *Sunrise, Sunset* at the wedding?"

"Can I drop catechism classes now?" my eleven-year-old daughter inquired hopefully.

"What about our Christmas tree?" asked my son of eight, who had overheard a discussion of Hanukkah.

I consulted with my husband-to-be. "No" to the meatballs. "Yes" to the song. Catechism classes were my decision. And, the kicker: he had to ask his mother about the Christmas tree. That was the first time he mentioned that decisions concerning our future might need to be checked out by his mother. It was not the last.

When my husband broached the topic, Ma was making noodle kugel in the kitchen. She leaned against the stove, as if a malady had attacked her entire body.

"You want to put up a what!?" Ma wailed.

"You are a Jewish boy!" (Norm was 46.)

"Do you know how this is killing me?" (He did.)

"If you love your mother, you will not do this thing." (He did it anyway, never told her and felt guilty the entire time.)

We approached the interfaith issue by deciding to have everything. We would have Easter egg hunts, Christmas Eve stockings and observance of Lent. We would also celebrate Hanukkah and Passover. Norm threw in a couple of others, Purim and Shavuot.

I wasn't sure what I was agreeing to, but the concept felt right and fair.

With Thanksgiving, Fourth of July and Memorial Day, the list of celebrations was growing. When we added birthdays, Christenings and Bar Mitzvahs, we would celebrate some event nearly every single week.

After we married, we considered buying stock in Hallmark. I sent cards to everyone on every holiday, including our rabbi at Christmas.

"This is a first," the rabbi told my husband.

"Rabbi, I can explain. Joy loves holidays and sends cards to everyone she likes."

"Did she send a Hanukkah card to the Pope?" the rabbi wanted to know.

I wanted to know everything about being Jewish—like sitting Shivah, candle lighting on the Sabbath and why rabbis could marry when priests couldn't.

I learned the words to *Dreidel, Dreidel*; and my husband learned the words to *Amazing Grace*.

He taught me about Menorahs and I taught him about the Trinity. I tried (and hated) Manischewitz. He sampled (and loved) my uncle's home-made wine. I taught him the meaning of rosary beads, he explained tefillin. He scanned the King James version of the Bible, I read Moses' interpretation of the Torah.

We were married under a huppah intertwined with flowers, he in his yarmulke, me in a veil. My uncle said the huppah looked a lot like the arbor in his backyard with the grapevines on top.

During the ceremony, my husband smashed a glass with his foot for good luck. My mother, thinking a chalice had dropped accidentally, ran under the huppah to pick up the sharp pieces before someone hurt themselves. The startled rabbi, who was just about to wish us Le Chayim! and Mazel Tov!, was speechless and never did get around to the marriage blessing.

It was an omen. Hence, the degree of luck in our marriage seemed foreordained.

It didn't seem so at first. As time went on, my brother began to hum *Sunrise, Sunset* on his way to work. My mother learned to make matzo balls. My daughter, after completing catechism classes, joined us occasionally at temple. My son transferred from his Catholic classes to a Hebrew school, finally making his Bar Mitzvah.

Working through our religious differences was a breeze compared to the other obstacles that surfaced during our short marriage. They were standard second-marriage complications, but they eventually overwhelmed us and we divorced. Sometimes best intentions just don't work out.

In the meantime, I learned a lot about being Jewish.

It's a lot like being Italian. There are celebrations, family get-togethers and traditions.

It's also a lot like being Catholic. Jews and Catholics belong to a congregation, attend services, contribute money, sing and pray, operate schools for their children and believe in God.

Major differences continue, of course, but my guess is that Moses probably didn't care what people wore on their heads or what songs they sang when he handed over God's Ten Commandments.

What I learned from being Jewish was to keep an open mind about all religions because we are probably more alike than not.

As long as we avoid the topic of Christmas trees.

8

Dishing Out Love

The Epsteins helped me learn that in our culturally diverse society there is never just one way. There are many ways. And that they are all valid, provided they lead—not to destruction—but to goodness, growth, gentleness and beauty.

Kathy Martin was not a typical cleaning lady. A 19-year-old dropout from Brown University, she decided to stay in Rhode Island instead of returning to her wealthy Miami family.

Why? We wondered. Cleaning windows and scrubbing sinks weren't exactly first choices for a rich, Waspy kid. But Kathy needed something to do while she decided how to indulge her fantasy of traveling to the Middle East.

"Daddy," a wealthy entrepreneur, was a stern Presbyterian deacon who called her at the office weekly, ordering her to come home. But Kathy wanted to trade in her silver spoon for a look at how real folks lived. She didn't know the doors it would open.

The call came in one busy Thursday morning.

"Do you do dishes?" an elderly male voice asked. He sounded like a crank, so I handed the phone to Denise, who had recently complained that her social life was so dull she would pay someone to make a crank call to her home.

"Here," I said, handing her the receiver, "save your money."

Mr. Epstein, it turned out, was legitimate. He wanted his house cleaned and his dishes washed—all four sets. "We have four of everything around here: four sets of pots, four drawers of silverware, everything. We have a kosher house. Do you know what that means?"

"No clue."

"It means we can't mix things up."

"Mister, look, this is some kind of joke, right?" Denise asked.

"No, really," he said. "My wife is laid up with the gout. Her toe is as big as a matzo ball and I don't feel so good myself. We have strict rules. We can't mix up the meat with the milk on the regular days, so we have dishes for that. Then we can't mix up the Passover food with the regular food, so we have dishes for that. So we have to switch the regular dishes and wash the ones that are..."

"Okay, I get the idea," interrupted Denise impatiently.

"Oy vey," he continued. "The whole thing gives me a headache. My wife even gives the dog separate dishes."

Since she was into new experiences, we decided to send Kathy to help Mr. Epstein. "Great," she said. "I'm dying to see a matzo ball toe."

She arrived at 8 the following morning. The house was cramped with worn, overstuffed furniture and there was a small TV in the corner of the living room.

"Come in, come in," he said. "You have to hurry so you can finish before sundown."

"We usually leave at three."

"That's fine. You must not be Jewish."

"Presbyterian."

"Oh. Well, our Sabbath begins this evening."

"Passover is coming," yelled Mrs. Epstein from the chair in another room. Kathy looked in to find a woman in a faded housecoat, her foot propped up on a mountain of cushions.

"Is it like Easter?" Kathy asked innocently.

"Certainly not," said Mrs. Epstein. "In ancient times, people made sacrifices each spring to ensure they would have a prosperous year."

"Like spring cleaning?" Kathy asked.

Mr. Epstein, who had been listening closely, said, "Yes. It's a lot like spring cleaning because it happens every spring and my grandchildren always clean me out of dollar bills."

"Oh, Harry," said Mrs. Epstein, who was taking Kathy's education very seriously, "would you knock it off already with the jokes? Dear, do you know why matzo is flat?" she continued, shooting Harry a threatening look. "Because when our people fled from the Pharaoh, no one had time to wait around for the bread to rise."

Kathy moved into the kitchen, wondering whether matzo was like the little wafers she ate in church, but deciding not to risk showing her ignorance. But when

Mrs. Epstein asked her to put seven chairs at the table after she had mentioned that six would be eating, Kathy decided she had to say something.

"Didn't you say that only six people were coming?"

"Have you ever heard of Elijah?"

"Uh, you mean the guy in the Bible?"

"No, dear," said Mrs. Epstein. "He's a prophet who will one day come back to bring peace to the world, so we set a place for him at the table each year in case he shows up."

"Why don't we just invite the girl to our Seder," Mr. Epstein interrupted, speaking as if Kathy weren't in the room.

"Good idea," Mrs. Epstein said approvingly.

Kathy returned to the shop that afternoon, delighted with her invitation. "My father would die if he knew I was going to a Passover dinner, but I can't wait. Except what happens if I do something stupid?" she asked excitedly, removing her Movado watch to wash her arms.

"They can't throw you out. You'd have to come back to clean the dishes," Denise cracked.

Kathy ignored her. "I might see Elijah. They're setting a place for him at the table in case he shows up."

"Does he come down the chimney, too?" Denise quipped. "And, by the way, I hope you're prepared to wear a beanie."

"That's for the men, you cultural illiterate," answered Kathy, who didn't dare tell Denise that only an hour before she had asked Mr. Epstein what the little black caps were used for. "You're just jealous because you weren't invited."

"Have a great time. I'd bring a pizza just in case."

Kathy arrived wearing her Sunday best: a pale lavender dress she had been saving for Easter and new, white pumps. When she entered the room, Mrs. Epstein was sitting on the couch in a bright red dress, beaming. The Epstein's son, Josh, and his wife and their two children were also there.

"So my father's trying to convert you," he said, smiling.

"What?" Kathy asked, holding her hands at her side. She didn't want to insult Josh.

"Just a joke. My parents love sharing Judaism with anyone who will listen. I see they talked you into coming."

They walked into the dining room, where an elaborately set table awaited them with a round plate in the center. It held an animal bone, an egg and some parsley, and flat, white crackers under a napkin.

Kathy thought about a pepperoni with mushrooms and cheese.

They all washed their hands at the table with a damp cloth. The Epsteins said some prayers she didn't understand while the children fidgeted impatiently.

They picked up blue books called Haggadahs and read about the history of the Jews. Then Mr. Epstein brought out real food—brisket of beef and a noodle dish she had never tasted.

Jacob, the four-year-old, searched for a matzo cracker, which he triumphantly dug from under the couch cushion. His grandfather picked him up, sat him on his lap and the family began to sing songs. When she rose at the end of the meal, Kathy's stomach felt like she had eaten for three.

"I feel like I'm leaving my family," she said, hugging Mrs. Epstein, who had slowly walked her to the door.

"Come over any time, dear," the lady said.

Back at the shop the next day, Kathy bounced in with a broad smile.

"So?" Denise asked.

"I think being Jewish is a lot more fun than being Presbyterian."

"Why?"

"Well, for starters, Elijah showed up—and he was a dead ringer for Kevin Costner."

9

The Older the Broom, the Softer the Straw

As the years went on, the business grew and grew. I lived in a house overlooking the bay and drove a convertible with an automatic lift-and-lower button. Life was good—until I went in for a routine physical checkup.

I read this Forrest Gump-like statement once: "Life is like an ice cream cone: Just when you think you've got it licked—it drips all over you." I realized that my time here could end at any moment and if I had any dreams on hold, I'd better get to them. This book is one of those dreams.

I also realized that, like books, our lives have many chapters, some exciting, or funny, or even blissful. Other chapters can be problematic, challenging, or downright scary. This complexity and diversity is what makes the Book of Life so rich. No portion can be skimmed over or skipped past if we are to experience its fullness and live it to the hilt.

As a cleaning lady, I got regular exercise mopping, dusting, scrubbing and sweeping.

But my body was changing daily, it seemed. For years, I had taken it for granted. It was just always there waiting for me when I woke up. I'd open my eyes, adjust to the light, look down and there it would be, just like I'd left it the night before, with all the pieces in good shape.

I'd wash it down, dress it up, pump a little java into it and head out...for 16,425 days it was like that. Then I turned 45. When I pulled back the covers the morning of my 45th birthday, I took a good long look at that body and realized that my birthday suit needed ironing.

My natural landscape had changed. Dimples were puckering on my rear end like potholes in a sandy road. Thin streaks of indigo veins threaded their way up my calves and thighs, crisscrossing and intersecting each other. Fleshy underarms were sagging with gravity. Rutted lines, like skid tracks, had chiseled new paths across my face. And my skin was shrinking and turning desert dry.

Other signs were emerging. I noticed that waking up, once a marvelous affair of rubbing my eyes and bounding downstairs, had become a somber affair of peeling my eyes open, pushing the snooze button, lying there for a while longer, shutting off the alarm, lying there for awhile, sitting up, then collapsing one leg over the side of the bed, waiting a few more minutes until everything else caught up, then dropping both feet into slippers that automatically propelled the body mass forward into the bathroom.

Day #16,425 was also the day I noticed that the first thing I did in the bathroom was spit. When did that start? What was I spitting out? I decided it must be dried out brain cells and maybe if I quit spitting, I could ward off dementia.

I also began to notice the sounds of involuntary body noises. An entire orchestra of popping and guttural clamor exploding haphazardly. Hoping to retire this off-key symphony, I called my chiropractor friend, Eddie Dulvaney.

"It's gas," he guessed. "It builds up when we get to a certain age. Nothing you can do about it."

To my horror, he also informed me that at "a certain age" the sphincter muscle begins to loosen up and the noises become less controllable. "Embarrassing as hell," he said, recalling his own recent experience in a cab on the way to a snazzy restaurant with a blind date.

I didn't like what I was hearing. So many changes associated with the "A" word. And phrases such as, "When you get to be our age" or, worse yet, "At your age..." Sometimes an endearment such as "Honey" was added, but no matter how people finessed the words, the "A" word sounded like an insult, an unnecessary count of how many days had piled up so far. The number of years I had inhabited the planet was nobody's business.

I guess what I really wanted was that no one would notice me aging. I didn't want it to show, did not want to be told that time had made me vulnerable to wrinkles.

In saner moments, it was poor health that aging represented, not an affront to my vanity. At least the sounds of aging—the creaks and sputters—weren't from illness.

That's when my doctor presented me with a reality check. That year's annual check-up happened to fall on my birthday. I prepared myself for the usual embarrassment and irritations, dismissing the "spotting" I'd recently noticed, assuming it was just a pre-menopausal inconvenience.

Before I could mention my birthday, the doctor stopped a routine abdominal check and began talking about "changes that occur about your age." The next sentence included "a rather large bump" in my lower abdomen that would require an X-ray. "Probably nothing," she assured me. "Some irregularities are common in the mid-forties."

I left her office and wondered how common people handled uncommon X-ray results. I found out a few days later when she called back.

"Your pelvic ultrasound test was abnormal," she said gently. At least she didn't say "dear."

"There is a cyst in your left ovary about the size of an orange. This may account for the unexplained bleeding."

I gasped. "Just to be on the safe side," she continued, "we'd like to do a biopsy and repeat the ultrasound in another thirty days. It's probably nothing." (Sure.) "Just your hormones going a little wacky around menopause time. So, try not to worry." (I had already worried myself into the shakes.) "Cysts and irregular bleeding occur often..."

At my age, I thought, finishing her sentence. So aging gracefully wasn't only about watching incremental physical deterioration. The scary stuff had arrived too soon. Orange-sized cysts spelled cancer to me. Irregular bleeding meant little time left. I felt my abdomen. Perhaps my little orange was quickly growing into a pumpkin.

But, this pumpkin was not for carrying off Cinderella, with Prince Charming in hot pursuit. The prince might chase someone *in* a pumpkin, but not someone *with* a pumpkin condition. Who would?

The cracked fairy tale would play just fine in my family, where all fear and tragedy was magically wanded away if it ever indeed existed. Even my grandpa, who I thought told me everything, had said not to worry when the doctor first told him he had a "bad" stomach. But that bad stomach kept getting worse until finally the doctor said there was nothing more he could do to fix it. Grandpa didn't talk about his bad stomach, didn't tell me it would just keep getting worse and did not tell me he would die.

In my family, illness was make-believe, not reality, never acknowledged out in the open. It was sometimes whispered, sometimes spelled out and sometimes called something else—never cancer—even though it had wiped out half the family. Given this background, my doctor's pronouncement that everything would be okay made me wonder what secret was being covered up.

I thought about all those things that week, the same week I realized that I spit in the mornings and that I might have cancer.

I realized mostly that I needed to call it what it was, if that was what it turned out to be. Not whisper it, not spell it, not call it something else. I needed to call it c-a-n-c-e-r. *Cancer*. Cancer! CANCER...cancer.

I needed to talk about what I had, *if* I had it. It was unfair not to talk about cancer, mine or anyone else's.

Everyone involved had a right to know. I would not steal from my children the opportunity to suffer with the sufferer and grieve the loss if it came to that.

I phoned them about the cyst, the ultrasound test and the scheduled biopsy. We cried together. We were scared together. We thought about how quickly change can occur.

We talked about cancer, what it is and what it does to people. We grieved over the possibilities of pain, suffering and loss.

What seemed at first like a death sentence became an unexpected awareness, a deep understanding of past confusion and pain about my grandpa, and an opportunity to reverse a family pattern.

And on the 16,447th day of my life, my children and I celebrated together when the results of the biopsy came back—negative.

My son showed me how to spit between my two front teeth. My daughter wanted to know if I wanted to meet her princely new neighbor.

I thought about what was important and what was not. Then I thought back to that time when Kim's second grade friends made fun of her mom being a cleaning lady and the advice I gave her then, "In God's economy nothing is wasted."

She never forgot. Because when I answered, "With my luck, this prince is probably a lousy dancer anyway. Or maybe I'm too old for him."

She challenged, "There are reasons for everything, Mom. Besides, what have you got to lose?"

The next night the prince and I went out. He was a fabulous dancer.

10

Sweeping a Street Corner Named "For Hire"

*Someone once said, "You can never really under-
stand a person until you crawl up inside their skin and
walk around in it a while." What we see on the outside,
many times, has little to do with what's on the inside.
Popeye always told us, "I am what I am." Lillian
taught me to take the time to get to know a person
while remembering "they are who they are."*

Sometimes we got frustrated with our work. We
cleaned for all kinds of people in all kinds of
situations: homes run by two men, one woman, foster
parents, adoptive parents and surrogate parents.

We were paid with alimony checks, rubber checks,
food stamps, dirty money, and a few times with funny
money.

Burnout is a problem in the cleaning business, too.
For a while Becky was infected. None of her customers
was fun anymore. Mr. Colebrook, the slob, continued to
leave toothpaste and nose hair in the sink. The Marino
kids never picked up their toys, and Becky tripped over
a plastic Army tank on the steps. "They take us for

granted," said Becky, a young mother who was working to help her husband start a business. "I'm sick of working for those people."

We certainly had unusual customers: circus clowns, mountain climbers and Clarice, a standard poodle whose owner used the poodle's trust fund to pay for cleaning her own room. Many times we saw people in the middle of change or crisis. We watched customers change addresses and last names, businesses and careers. We even watched one of our customers, thirty-one-year-old Lillian Lutweigler, change all four at the same time.

Lillian, whose divorce had just become final, moved out of a four-bedroom home in an upscale suburb across town, into a renovated 2-bedroom duplex with her four-year-old daughter, Jenny.

Shortly after settling into her new digs, Lillian changed jobs and acquired a new professional name. Lillian Lutweigler, former data processing clerk at Thermidoro's Plumbing Supply Center, became "Luscious," a lunchtime exotic dancer at the Foxy Dame. According to the electronic billboard outside, the act wasn't tame: "Luscious Lil Lets It All Hang Out At Lunchtime."

"I wanted to start my life over," she told Becky, as she stretched to pull back a curtain at the window of her new place. "I took a long look at my life. I was thirty-one years old and bored silly, except for Jennie."

"I was tired of typing up packing slips for copper tubing. Tired of cooking boring dinners for my alcoholic husband, Ted. Tired of being tired of it all. I needed a change," she said that afternoon.

"So you quit work, just like that?" Becky asked.

"I quit my entire life. Just like that," she said, snapping her fingers. "And I went off into the bright lights."

She went into the lights, all right. Up Route 95 North into the city, where the *Providence Journal* ad read, "Exciting daytime work, unbelievable money, no experience necessary. Apply in person."

The Dame was just off the highway in an inner-city neighborhood with used furniture stores, pawn shops and wholesale jewelry stores. The building was warehouse sized, its parking lot tucked away off the main road.

Lillian told Becky how she parked the station wagon and stuffed an extra pen in her briefcase in order to fill out an application.

There was no application.

"Know how to dance?" the burly, whiskered man behind the bar asked, after looking her up and down and scratching his chin.

"Sure," said Lillian. She was always the first up to line-dance at weddings. She had taught Ted how to slow dance in one night, and won a twist contest in high school. While she described her dance repertoire, the man behind the bar reached down and pulled out something blue and frilly and dangled it in front of Lillian.

"Okay, okay, you're hired. Show up tomorrow. Here's your uniform." He threw her the shimmery blue material.

She held it between her two fingers, arm stretched out, dangling it like a Christmas ornament. The long tassels bounced and the sequins glittered.

"Sorry. I'm not about to wrap this around my body.

I don't want to be anyone's holiday surprise."

She dropped the tassels on the bar and picked up her purse. The man had turned his back to her and wiped glasses above his head.

"The girls make five hundred dollars a day," he said casually.

She plucked up the blue thing and ran a quick calculation through her mind: Jenny's school tuition, rent, utilities, phone, food, car payments. "When can I start?"

"Tomorrow. You'll do the noon-hour show."

As Lillian told the story, Becky was organizing Lillian's underwear, which consisted of white cotton bras and briefs.

"Isn't this pretty tame for a stripper?" Becky teased.

"I'm not a stripper. I'm an exotic dancer," protested Lillian, waving a red satin thong, trimmed in eyelet at the waistband.

"Uh, Lillian, where's the other half?"

"There isn't any," replied Lillian.

"Wow," said Becky, fascinated, "don't you ever get a little chilly?"

"Sometimes," laughed Lillian, "but there is usually so much hot air around there, I rarely notice the temperature."

"Who ARE those guys?" Becky asked.

"You would be amazed," said Lillian. "I used to think only sleazebags went to these places, but just last week at lunchtime, the president of my credit union tried to stuff a five-dollar bill inside my bikini.

"Maybe what you do isn't that sleazy," offered Becky hesitantly.

"I bump and grind to blaring music, shaking tassels on top of tables bought by guys like Mr. Credit Union President."

"Why would someone buy a table?" Becky wondered innocently.

"They don't actually buy them, they rent them. It's forty bucks for the hour and they sit there looking up at me dancing."

"Why don't they just rent a Madonna video and save about thirty-five bucks?"

"We create an atmosphere of erotica," Lillian explained, pouting her lips and striking a burlesque pose. "It's all a fantasy, a mirage, make-believe. These guys swig down a couple of beers on their lunch break, pretend they're Joe Stud and throw money around. Then they swagger out smiling and go back to the office. When anyone asks them why their cheeks are flushed, they say they've been taking the stairs instead of the elevator for exercise. See?"

"I guess."

"Nobody gets hurt. They get some lunchtime kicks. I make a few bucks. Jenny gets a Schwinn for Christmas. Everybody comes out a winner. Simple, right?" Lillian sat down at her dresser and folded her arms across her chest.

It didn't seem simple to Becky, who was trying to picture Lillian Lutweigler—Jenny's mom, Ted's ex-wife, and former data processing clerk at Thermidoro's Plumbing Supply Center—in those tassels.

"Aren't you ever embarrassed?" she asked timidly.

Lillian straightened up the makeup and perfume on her dresser, shut the closet door and sank into the living room couch, thinking a long time about that question.

When she answered, finally, the cynical Luscious was nowhere in sight. Lillian Lutweigler was back and suddenly seemed very tired.

She looked at Becky, uncrossed her arms and said in a soft voice, "Of course I'm embarrassed. You think it's easy getting up there in this?" She pulled a royal blue sequined thong out from under the couch cushion and held it up. "I used to be too embarrassed to wear something like this to the beach. Now I willingly gyrate in this getup for a bunch of slobbering drunks. It's sure different from Thermidoro's all right. How much job satisfaction do you think I have, huh?" she said to no one in particular, her voice shaking. "Do you think I enjoy waking up in the morning, dropping Jenny off at school, saying hello to all the other moms, then heading out to my gig?"

Nervous that she had pushed her interrogation too far, Becky said nothing, afraid to move.

"Look," Lillian said quietly, "I don't mean to sound so angry. But things got all mixed up. I got married right out of high school, never dated anyone except Ted. At some point I figured I'd missed out on the bright lights, the excitement. Ted started drinking. I got bored with being a shipping clerk. You know, the old "grass looks greener" story."

She shook her head solemnly, "Ha," she continued. "I added pizzazz all right. I pizzazzed myself right into dancing on tabletops in G-strings and pasties to make a living. But no matter what happens now, the fact is, I made the choice and I am living with it and making the best out of it all. I have Jenny to think about and I never want her to go without. Do you know what it's like to be a single mom?"

Becky shook her head.

"It's tough. I need the money and the money is real good there. So right now, I do what I have to do, that's all. No sense complaining about it. It's a job, period," she said, looking at her watch. "It's time to go to work."

Luscious stuffed a pair of five-inch royal blue sequined heels into a tote bag along with her royal blue sequined thong, a couple of blue fringed tassels, some makeup and dashed out the door.

Becky finished cleaning the living room. She looked at her watch. It was noon when she walked into Jenny's room to straighten it up, about the same time Luscious would be starting her act.

The room didn't need much work. The Snow White bedspread was neatly tucked into each corner and the Seven Dwarfs smiled, sneezed and grumped their way across Jenny's pillows.

Sitting atop the pillows were Jenny's two closest friends—Teddy the Bear and Bubbles the Frog, a brown, pop-eyed stuffed animal. Bubbles' legs were worn and soft stuffing peeked out. On the pink and white nightstand were several books piled neatly one on top of the other. Jenny was learning from her mommy about *The Velveteen Rabbit*, *The Emperor's Clothes* and *The Cat In The Hat*.

Nearby was a note:

To my little angel, Jenny,

> *I know you are scared right now.*
> *Change is always scary. But we are*

*going to be okay and pretty soon
everything will seem happy again.
I promise.*

I love you,

Mommy

Becky held the card. Now she understood why Lil had become Luscious. She recalled how often she had complained about hauling the vacuums from house to house, how impatient she had been when customers pointed out a spot here and there. She thought about the times she had come home exhausted but found that Al had made dinner. She wondered what her feet would feel like after wearing stilettos instead of Nikes all day. She thought about those moments when life held nothing more than diapers, formula and car pooling, times when being husbandless and childless, seemingly without concern for reputation, might seem like fun for a week or two.

Now she had a sense of what that would really be like.

Back at the office, Denise was struggling to roll a carpet cleaner through the door.

"I'm definitely finding a new job," Denise threatened.

"A lot of people have it worse. Try dancing on a table top in tassels and five-inch stilettos."

"Huh?"

"See ya," Becky said, heading out the door.

11

Unclutterizing Clutter

The cleaning business grew and grew and became one of the largest of its kind in the Northeast. The money started to roll in and I started to buy many new things. It suddenly became important to keep up with the Joneses...the Smiths...and anyone else in the neighborhood who had more than I did. I became a possession junkie, flashing my new-found success like a neon sign.

A shift in satisfaction started to occur. The more I had, the more I wanted. For so many years I'd lived a simple, uncomplicated life without things. Now my life seemed crowded and confused. Then I met a man who taught me about the things that really matter in life. He helped me get back to basics and realize that no matter who we are, some things are more important than others.

My life is simplified again. I got rid of the internal and external clutter. In the process I discovered that peace had filled the newly prepared spaces.

I met a man a few years ago who taught me about taking time to smell the roses. The man was the movie star, Vincent Gardenia, the eccentric character actor who played Cosmo Castorini, Cher's cheating father in *Moonstruck.*

We met, by chance, after I hired someone to manage the cleaning company so I could try my hand at writing. Years before, I had dreamed of becoming a journalist. Although life's path had veered off in another direction, the dream never completely faded.

I decided to begin writing about local people, specifically people of my own Italian-American heritage. So, armed with a pocket-recorder and notepad, I would stroll down DePasquale Avenue or into Christopher Columbus Square, following aromas of Parmesan and garlic, into trattorias, barber shops and fruit markets, nurturing the cultural roots that took hold long ago. I spent time visiting with the gentle souls who lived in the neighborhood, relaxing and reminiscing at sidewalk tables while sipping espresso or nibbling on cannolis.

At home, I'd type up the stories and send them off to several small ethnic newspapers. In time, my interviews began appearing regularly while the interviewees became neighborhood stars. Excited relatives snatched up copies by the armful and sent them to all corners of the globe.

One day I received a call from the editor of a large Italian magazine in New Jersey.

"My Aunt Mary has a friend, who has a cousin in Rhode Island, who keeps telling her about your stories. They sound pretty interesting," he said. "How about doing some interviews for us?"

"Sure. What neighborhood do you want me to start with?"

"Brooklyn. And, oh yeah, can you start tomorrow?"

It turned out their regular reporter, scheduled to interview an actor, was sick. Could I be in New York City the next morning at 10:00 a.m.?

Transportation wasn't my concern. Interviewing a movie star was. Sipping espresso with a local pizza parlor owner was one thing, but interviewing Vincent Gardenia... another. I was petrified, but took down all the information and said I'd be there somehow.

I took the bus from Rhode Island to the Port Authority at dawn the next morning, where I called Mr. Gardenia for directions. He actually answered the phone. "You have to take a taxi here," he said, "but make sure those bums don't overcharge you." Well, apparently the bums did, and he had a fit.

That's what's wrong with this country," he said, shaking his head as he let me in the front door. "Everybody's taking advantage of everybody else." I stood in his living room, coat still on, briefcase in hand, frozen as I watched him pace back and forth across his worn brown carpet, shaking his fist at human greed.

When he finally stopped pacing, he motioned me to the couch, with, "Oh, I'm sorry. I get carried away. Please make yourself comfortable."

Nervously, I set the microphone on the arm of his chair, took a seat across from him and listened for the next hour as he spoke about his acting career. Occasionally, I mumbled questions he'd probably heard and answered dozens of times. But, with each question, he enthusiastically filled in the blanks.

This passion was the driving force in every aspect of

Vincent Gardenia's life, on stage and off, and helped shape him into one of America's greatest character actors.

He certainly didn't look like a matinee idol. And he hadn't called the wardrobe department to prepare for my visit. He wore a faded green Banlon shirt that was stretched to its limit over his big belly. His brown polyester pants were hitched up somewhere underneath his stomach falling flat in the rear. He wore no shoes, and one sock needed a few stitches in the heel.

His legs were thick and short, his body beefy. I asked him about *Moonstruck*, the movie that won him an Oscar nomination.

"We all got along great. Olympia Dukakis, Cher, the whole crew. It was a fun movie to make because I could relate to the Dean Martin music, pasta marinara and family interference. It brought back a lot of memories for Danny Aiello, Nicholas Cage and me."

He gazed out the front window, taking in the two-family houses across the street, the miniature front lawns and the Chinese couple pushing a baby carriage. His map-lined face softened into a relaxed youthfulness as he relived another time.

"I remember growing up in this neighborhood," he said. "We were all Italians. The butcher, the shoemaker, everybody. The houses on Seventy-seventh Street in Brooklyn, where we first moved, were all attached. All the clothes were hanging on lines from porch to porch, and we could talk from our windows to the neighbors. Everybody looked out for one another. It was wonderful. The neighborhood was part of the family."

Deeply committed to serving that larger family,

young Vincent and his father presented plays for the Italians on the block and beyond. "We used to work the Italian community in the five boroughs. One-, two- and three-night stands," he recalled. "We would bring the Italian language and Italian sentiments to these small towns and to these people who missed their villages. They were so appreciative. I climbed on the stage when I was five years old and I've hardly stepped off since."

In those 65 years on stage, television and in film, Vincent Gardenia played an estimated 500 parts and won many awards.

He was loved by Americans, honored by Presidents and respected by people in his industry, not only because of his talent, but because he was a simple, unassuming man who clung to the values of his culture. He didn't want things to change from the way he remembered them as a boy.

"C'mere," he said, motioning.

He took me down the narrow stairway to a paneled basement with photographs signed by Cher, DeNiro, Bronson and other luminaries. The shelves were crammed with dusty plaques and tarnished trophies. Movie posters were rolled up and stuck in any available space. I was star-struck and walked around in a daze from one piece of Hollywood history to another, the notepad dangling from my hand. I mumbled something sophomoric like, "Aren't you afraid they'll get mildewed down here?" He stopped for a moment, taking me in for the first time.

"Is this your first story?" he asked.

I thought about lying, but nodded and croaked,

"Sort of."

He let out a giant laugh, barely able to catch his breath. I felt like a rookie reporter and a rookie adult.

He wiped his eyes with the back of his hand.

"I started out with nuthin' too. That's how you gotta do it sometimes," he said sympathetically.

He motioned for me to follow him. "If you want to find out what my life's really about, let's go outside," he said, leading the way back upstairs and through the kitchen.

We stepped onto a concrete patio that was about 10-feet square. There was a plastic-covered picnic table in the center and a small rusty gas grill in the corner.

Three edges of the patio were lined with rich soil where eight neatly staked and tied tomato plants stood proudly displaying their offspring. A small mint bush grew close by.

This was the portrait of Vincent Gardenia I could paint for my readers. A man standing quietly in his backyard city garden looking at his tomatoes, at the clothesline suspended from his neighbor's porch and, finally, at me.

"This is what it's all about. Not the awards or the fame or the photographs. When I come out here to water my tomatoes, I'm back on our farm in Naples, where everything was simple to understand."

Then he leaned down and broke off a piece of mint and handed it to me. "Smell that," he said. "Is there anything more beautiful?"

I peered at this man standing on his concrete patch, who could close his eyes and drift back to a simpler, less complicated place in time. I remembered how terrified I had been just thinking about meeting him today, how intimidated I'd been by his fame, how I'd worried that we'd have absolutely nothing in common. Yet, out there on that tiny patio, on a still July afternoon in Brooklyn, we connected—person to person, soul to soul—through a tiny miracle of God's creation.

I took in a long deep breath, inhaling the sweet aroma of the mint leaf in my hand. Was there anything more beautiful?

I couldn't think of a single thing.

12

Garlic—The Universal Solvent

What seems so possible to dreamers, often seems impossible to their friends and family. I've found, however, that the universe is on the dreamer's side. When I decided to sing, new people began to appear in my life who could help, songs I needed became available, and opportunities opened up seemingly from nowhere. I've read that when we leap, the net always appears.

This experience taught me about change and how necessary it is for us to grow and become all the universe intended us to be even when others are skeptical. When the Great Housekeeper in the sky asks me, "Well, Joy, what did you do with the melody I gave you?" I can now say, "I belted it out in a little cabaret in New York City."

I was 45 when I decided to expand my talents beyond house-cleaning and become a cabaret singer in New York City.

"You want to do what?" my 75-year-old mother asked.

I told her I wanted to drape myself over a grand piano in a smoky club in Manhattan and sing *It Had To Be You.* She felt my forehead.

"Why not?" I asked her. "I sang when I was five. Why can't I sing now?"

"That was forty years ago!" she reminded me.

So, what's a few decades here or there?

Being a cabaret singer had been my dream since I was five and saw a torch singer belting a Sophie Tucker-type number from deep within her gold lamé gown. I also heard Connie Francis, that beloved Italian girl, sing her heart out. However, I didn't want to sing numbers like *Stupid Cupid, Where The Boys Are* and, oh yes, her rendition of *Mama,* a weepy Italian litany that made her mother cry. But my mother was persuasive in a way that Jewish and Italian mothers understand: "If you love me, you'll sing this song to your mama," she told her five-year-old.

So, I did. In Italian. Tears and all.

On Sunday afternoons, all the neighbors came to cry while I sang. The Pisaturro's came from next door. They brought their cousins, the Marciano's. Marie Santo Pietro, my best friend, brought our mutual boyfriend, Ronnie Del Nero. My Uncle Angelo, from Providence, brought his fianceé, Dolly, and I brought my own dolly, named Anna, who let me cry and hug her on those Sundays.

My mother cooked food for the event, which was drenched in garlic, of course: breakfast, lunch and dinner, not to mention in-between meal snacks. Garlic bread and fried eggs; garlic and salami sandwiches on crusty Italian bread soaked in olive oil; and garlic pork chops with garlic spinach. Germs and vampires didn't have a chance at our house. Neither did fresh breath. So, each Sunday afternoon, when we revved up *Oh, Sole Mio*, our cat, Sylvester, left the house.

I was 45 when I decided to make a comeback. If Connie Francis could do it, why not me?

I found a singing teacher in Boston who agreed to accompany me on songs like *Moon River*. My next teacher would be in New York.

I packed for the Big Apple, my friends solidly behind me:

"Are you crazy?"

"You'll embarrass your children!"

"You're too old now!"

"You need years of training!"

"You don't know anybody in New York City."

I went anyway. Every Tuesday, I'd pack two salami-and-cheese sandwiches, a piece of fruit, a couple of Diet Pepsi's and hop on the 7:15 a.m. Bonanza bus from Providence to New York City. It cost $29.95 one way and took $3 1/2$ hours. It didn't matter. I would have commuted to Saturn.

I always sat in the front seat, where I could talk to the bus drivers. On my very first trip I met Ralph, who had one year, two months and 16 days left until retirement.

Then I met Bill, who had a lisp, "You get dithcovered yet?" he would always ask.

And Tony, an Italian waiter, who brought his own salami sandwiches.

I also met Pete, the guy who threw the baggage into the compartments on the side of the bus. "Let me know when you need someone to carry your bags in the city," he offered.

And Sam, the greeter. Sam didn't work for the bus company, but he hung around the terminal and appointed himself the official greeter to every traveler. "Have a nice trip now. Nice seeing you. Careful getting up them steps." And for me, "Step aside, now. Let the movie star get on board."

Unfortunately, the New York City club owners didn't care that I was Queen of the Bus Terminal because not one of them gave me a chance to audition.

"I'm a singer," I said.

"So's every other dame that walks in here."

Then Fate led me to the office of Stanley Moyer, a booking agent for a garish little club on West 46th Street called Don't Tell Mama.

"What do you do?" he asked. The club looked like a smoky, B-movie set: long tables with chairs, dimmed lights, faded velvet curtains and a pool hall in the back.

"I sing *Mama* in Italian," I said.

He showed me the dressing room, a dusty, messy little room with a torn couch, located at the bottom of a rickety flight of stairs in the basement. A lone light bulb hung from a cord.

"It's fabulous," I squeaked shakily.

"Great!" he said. "When can you start?"

"Any time," I answered. "The bus runs seven days a week."

Three weeks later, for my debut, Bonanza Bus Lines had to add an extra bus to their 7:15 a.m. run from Providence to New York to carry all the friends and family who had cried and applauded in our living room 40 years earlier. Ralph drove and Sam came along for a free ride. He spent his entire $3 1/2$ hours walking up and down the aisles greeting everyone.

My mother sat up front and Uncle Angelo sat in the back with Dolly. In between was everyone else left from the old Sunday afternoon crowd. The Pisaturro's, the Marciano's, Marie (who had long ago stolen Ronnie away from me and now had a Ronnie, Jr.) and 68 other relatives and friends. Of course, each had brought a little something along for the ride: spinach pies with garlic, pepperoni pizza with garlic and scungilli salad with garlic. "Mangia, mangia," everyone shouted.

Mrs. Angelini remembered to bring the Wet Naps so we could wipe the olive oil and fingerprints off the bus's vinyl seats. Uncle Angelo remembered to bring two coolers of his homemade wine.

Sam, the greeter, got smashed and passed out. Uncle Ricardo begged my mother to do the Tarantella right there in the aisle of the #48 Bonanza Bus.

Ralph dropped us off at West 46th and 8th, and we all filed out, or rather, poured out of the bus, reeking of garlic and drenched in olive oil. As we walked through the front door of Don't Tell Mama, the waiting crowd gasped and held their breath.

It was an Italian invasion. A party in the making for 40 years.

We yelled. We fought. We kissed everybody in the place.

I headed down the stairs and rehearsed for 20 minutes. Then I poured myself into a gold lamé gown, threw a feather boa over my shoulder, and climbed back up the shaky stairs, hoping my dress wouldn't rip and my nervousness wouldn't show.

My act was called, "The Last of the Red Hot Mamas." I trembled nervously for a few seconds, but then I looked out at my extended family. They were smiling. There was no way I could fail. I vamped down from the stage, ran my boa over Mr. Pisaturro's face, then I crawled on top of the grand piano and began to lustily croon *It Had To Be You*.

Over the thunderous applause, my mother hollered, "Connie, baby, eat your heart out."

13

Life in a Vacuum Sucks

Since I never got around to a formal education, I make each day an informal classroom for knowledge. I see the world as a gigantic, wondrous, exciting mystery and I want to learn everything possible. I read and read. Sometimes it's Thoreau or Emerson and, yes, sometimes it's the <u>Enquirer</u>.

Scoffed at by intellectuals, the *National Enquirer* offers the rest of us a kaleidoscope of current events, gossip and fun. At our cleaning shop, the latest edition always sat in the middle of our coffee table, with old issues neatly stacked below.

We lusted our way through each page, peering into the bedrooms of Hollywood's cheatingest couples: Kevin Costner's alleged romp with a Hawaiian dancer, Kelsey Grammar's newest affair and Roseanne's marriage to her bodyguard. We delighted in their transgressions, pondered their fates in and out of divorce courts, and fell with them into the arms of others.

This was a typical Monday morning meeting: we

always hit the important stuff before the business stuff.

You might think we were fluff-heads. Well, I admit, I was mostly interested in the gossip. But my friends read the paper for other sections. Stacey read it strictly for "the articles," specifically, the celebrity recipes. She swore by the dishes of the month, like Shirley MacLaine's vegetarian omelet and Cher's oven-roasted burritos. There was this week's fish chowder, "a classic recipe from the Massachusetts politician." Ted Kennedy's smiling face had been pasted on the ingredients list between the salt pork and the butter. Every week she clipped those recipes out and taped them into a notebook. When her professor husband, Stan, started asking where they came from, she answered "my mother," then promptly began to cloister the book in her underwear drawer, beneath the push-up bras.

Perhaps I'm one of the few unabashed fans of the *Enquirer*. Don't ask me about the other tabloids—I'd never trust anything they say. But there must be some reason why the *Enquirer* is so popular. I think it's the brazenness of their reporters. They stop at nothing to get a story. Enraged story subjects have punched them out, smashed their cameras and chased them down by car. Reporters regularly endure libel suits so people like me can get to appreciate their chutzpa on a weekly basis.

Our accountant, Max O'Donnell, read the paper for its jokes. He clipped and memorized them, recounting them for frustrated clients at tax time.

"I've got a joke for you..." he liked to open.

This was his favorite: "A lady of the evening goes up to this guy who's in his eighties and says, 'I'll do anything you want for fifty dollars.' The old guy thinks about this for a minute, then opens his car door, lets her in, and starts to drive off. After they drive a while, she says to him, 'Hey, Pops, where do you think you're taking me?'

He turns to her and says, 'I'm taking you home to paint my garage.' "

Max swears his jokes have won him clients.

In Rhode Island, the *Enquirer* reached a certain Newport drug store three whole days ahead of the supermarkets. Many fans thought nothing of driving 20 miles and paying $1.69 for updates on everything from Hollywood to the supernatural.

Men didn't understand the *Enquirer*. Take Matt, the man I was seeing at the time. He was an open-minded, liberated male who supported my growth in every way. Matt and I prided ourselves on having an honest relationship with each other. We read *Men Are From Mars, Women Are From Venus* and learned how to discuss issues clearly, without fear of rejection or misunderstanding. We accepted each other unconditionally, despite our differences—except where the *Enquirer* was concerned.

"How can you read that trash?" he asked after dinner one evening, as I pored over a story detailing the real reason for Julia Roberts' divorce.

"It's not trash," I retorted. "You would be amazed at what I learn every week."

"Yeah, right," he said. "What is it this week? Three-headed hairy babies born during the sun's eclipse to a chimpanzee and a collie?"

There was no use trying to explain my allegiance,

which Matt called an obsessive compulsion. The paper was misunderstood. Why did so many people thumb their noses at it and treat it with such disrespect?

Some articles had enough substance to be featured in any public school's current events classes. The paper was colorful, graphically pleasing, aesthetic and magazine-pretty.

But because of intellectual snobs like Matt, I became neurotic about buying the paper in public. Maybe it was my imagination, but bystanders seemed to smirk when I laid it down on the checkout counter. Once a new drugstore clerk picked it up, read a headline, looked at me and burst out laughing.

I became more careful. I would wait for the lines to clear, avoid the clerk's eyes and, if I were cornered, tell people with a sigh of resignation, that it was for my aunt, daughter, sister—anyone but me. Then I would sneak it home and hide it in a file that read "Taxes: 1977."

Matt knew me pretty well. He knew about my teenage romp with Eddie D'Mitri in Eddie's Ford Fairlane and about that mole on my lower back that I covered up with Clearasil in the summer.

He knew that I would henna over the gray hair every three weeks, and that vanilla ice cream gave me gas, but he never knew, as long as we were together, that I still bought the *National Enquirer* every single week. After all, you can't live life in a vacuum.

The way I looked at it, "Enquiring minds" did not *always* need to know.

14

Dissolving Sticky Situations

I read somewhere that women are the glue in our society. We are the gender that holds broken, damaged pieces together and mends them, if they are mendable. One of our greatest gifts seems to be a relentless dedication to finding solutions to problems, whether it's our child falling behind in school or our marriage falling apart. Donna helped me see this blessing in action.

Donna whispered "Guess who's coming to dinner?" into Nancy's ear one Monday afternoon as she was changing the belt on her vacuum.

"Donna, why are you whispering?" Nancy asked, wiping her hands on her jeans. "If it's your brother-in-law and he calls you 'Debbie' again, try to act like an adult. No name tag at the table this time, okay?"

"No, no," Donna said, smirking.

"Okay," said Nancy, "let's see. It probably isn't Mother Teresa. I heard she's been fasting for world peace. And John Gotti is having his meals brought in these days."

"More interesting than that," Donna said smirking. "It's my ex!"

"Donna's ex is coming to dinner," yelled Nancy to the rest of us, who crowded around. We hadn't heard this story and it sounded like juicy *National Enquirer* stuff.

Tell us about the divorce, we begged, salivating for a good tale.

"Steve's a doctor now."

We raised our eyebrows and licked our chops.

"And you divorced him!" teased Denise. "I'd say your timing was a little off."

"He was a medical student when we were married. But it wasn't much of a marriage. He was away a lot, and whenever he had any time, he would go to meetings he didn't need to be at. I finally kicked his butt out after he missed dinner for the hundredth time."

"Don't student doctors work all the time?"

"Yeah, but that's when they're single. I wanted to get pregnant, but he didn't even have time for that. We started growing apart."

"Ted and I used to have that problem. We got so busy with work and the kids that we never had time together," volunteered Nancy. "We finally figured out a solution."

"What did you do?"

"I would take the kids to my sister's for the night. We would have a candlelight, canned-chili dinner like we used to. Ted would put on Roy Orbison and I would put on something silky. The next morning things were a lot clearer."

"That was different," said Donna sadly. "There

were other problems."

I tried not to seem eager to hear more gossip.

"We moved here from the Heartland. You guys don't know this, but I was raised on a farm with pigs and a rooster named Shut-Up-Will-Ya who woke me every morning at six. When I got up, I would look out my window to cornfields that stretched all the way to tomorrow. I've been really homesick. I miss the solitude."

"Why are you still here?" Denise wanted to know.

"I invested the little money I had in a lobster boat and lost it all. I needed to earn some money before I left. That was two years ago."

"So why don't you try Nancy's cure?"

"It's probably too late," Donna said, unconvincingly. "Although I guess I could make corn fritters for a start."

"Why corn fritters?"

"It's sort of how we started out. So many soft Nebraska Sunday afternoons sitting on a blanket under the big tree, munching corn fritters I fried up for him each week. Everything was uncomplicated. He talked about how he would be a doctor some day and I talked about how I would follow him to Timbuktu. It seems we just got very caught up in it all those last five years," she told Donna.

"To tell you the truth, I would trade this rat race in a minute for just one afternoon in the soft Nebraska sun in the clearing by the river. Canned chili, huh?" she asked mulling it over in her mind.

The next day, Donna left a message on our answering service at 5 a.m., long before anyone came in.

"I don't have anything scheduled today and I don't

want you to schedule me for anything this week. Steve and I are going to Nebraska for a few days. Maybe it was Roy Orbison or maybe it was the silk. Whatever it was it did the trick.

Roy still sounds great these days and Steve couldn't get enough of my...corn fritters."

15

Welcoming Mustard Stains

Auntie Mame said, "Life is a banquet and most people are starving to death." Thelma Howard taught me that at Life's banquet, one of the main ingredients is fun. Kicking up our heels __in__ life helps keep us from kicking our heels __at__ life.

Where was I when Walt Disney advertised for a cleaning lady?

I know where Thelma Howard was. She was chain-smoking while thumbing through the classifieds when she spotted Walt's ad. The rest, as they say, is history. She called for an interview, got hired, and for the next thirty years she cooked dinners for Walt and the gang, washed their dirty socks, and kept things humming along. She became part of the Disney family and they loved her.

Thelma, who the family called Fou-Fou, died a few years ago with $8.5 million dollars worth of Disney stock tucked away neatly in a shoe box—accumulated gifts from birthdays and holidays.

What extraordinary housekeeping skills did

Thelma possess to win a place in the Disney family's hearts? In the news clipping Walt's daughter, Diane, explained. "Thelma was fun. She always made sure the refrigerator was filled with hot dogs."

Hot dogs! She gives them hot dogs and they give her 8.5 million bucks? Either there was something special in those hot dogs or Fou-Fou stumbled across one of life's greatest secrets:

> It isn't what's being served on the table of Life
> that matters.
> What counts is how we dish it up.

I discovered, thanks to Thelma, that what unites a family isn't gourmet dinners by candlelight, but small, happy, shared times together—hot-dog-and-bean moments.

Frankfurters were never the first things I thought of when I needed cheering up. I served them to my children over the years, with an extra helping of guilt, because many times that was all we could afford. I apologized my way through all-beef, skinless, kosher and kielbasa. Made amends over Ballpark's 99-cent franks, and even (when times got a little bit easier), Nathan's $2.99 a package, never thinking for a moment about banquet blessings.

But there was something special about Thelma's franks that inspired Uncle Walt to dispense those stock certificates. My guess is that he looked forward to the simplicity of those hot dog nights after a long day of dream building.

I imagined Thelma making a big deal of those

nights—decorating the kitchen, throwing a weenie party, a picnic, a celebration.

I pictured her bursting through the swinging kitchen doors, complete with white chef's hat, party apron, and mustard stains. She'd be carrying a steaming platter of hot dogs while the Disney children squirted mustard all over their paper plates like the Toontown characters they grew up with. The plates wouldn't be the heavy-duty kind, but thin orange ones with fluted edges that got soaked through and leaked.

And balloons. Thelma would have lots of balloons. Pink, blue and magenta ones on the backs of each chair, and a few tied to a napkin holder on the table. She knew about celebrating the simplest things in life, about laughter, about friendship, about sharing.

I was sorry that I had given too few of these times to my children. For us, hot dogs meant mom was scrimping again to pay the rent or rushing to get dinner over with quickly...again. They'd always hurry through, never complaining and never savoring, as glad as I was to get the whole thing over with. I never encouraged conversation and didn't want to hear any. They usually ate meals silently while sitting with trays in front of the television.

My example, unfortunately, came from my childhood. Dinner at our house was a solemn affair. My father sat at the head of the table and insisted on total silence while he ate. So instead of sharing the events of our day, instead of laughter and friendship, we sat quietly, chewing and swallowing, our eyes looking down.

I remember each miserable moment sticking in my throat like the food that didn't want to go down. The only time we talked at the table was on holidays, when the calendar said we were allowed—and we were expected—to enjoy the food, companionship and conversation. I don't know where that tradition of silence came from but I remember how I dreaded dinnertime.

I also don't understand why I chose to repeat such a despised family tradition. But I had. However, one great thing about life is that we can reinvent it whenever and however we want. So one day I decided to start doing dinners Thelma Howard's way.

I started by bringing home a dining room table.

"What's that?," Mark asked as I pulled a chair from its cardboard crate.

"A chair," I said, "there are five others just like this one. They all sit around a table."

It was a bit rocky at first. I had decided we should become a dinner-focused family at the very time my adolescents were out to lunch, pulling away into their own worlds. But I forged ahead and they adapted.

I dusted off the stove, turned it on and began to cook up a storm. New smells floated through the rooms. Simmering tomato sauce with sweet basil, chocolatey cookies with M&M's, fresh crusty bread, freshly squeezed orange juice. It all went from the stove to the table, and each night we sat down together and talked.

After we got into the pattern, I learned things about my children I never knew: Mark's desire to become a forest ranger (although he had never stepped foot in a forest, he thought Smokey the Bear's job was pretty cool). And my daughter's desire to study art and Italian men (not necessarily in that order) in Florence some day.

We began to look forward to our scheduled times together and took turns cooking. Mark became the Omelet King and Kim was the Pasta Princess. My lasagna became known throughout the neighborhood and we all pitched in together during our celebrated hot dog and beans parties.

Now, years later, as I look back at our lives during that time, I am so grateful for Thelma's example. She helped my children and me develop a joyous ritual and grow closer to each other. Although we now live apart, when we do get together, restaurants are out of the question.

Thelma, if you're listening, thanks for teaching me that whenever life serves us wieners, we should throw a wiener party!

Eight and a half million bucks?

"Just for the record, Thelma...I think you were underpaid."

16

Polishing Metals, Medals and Mettle

I've never fought in a war, but I have experienced fear. I've had bouts with it on and off over the years. Thoreau said, "Nothing is so much to be feared as fear." It is always waiting for me, just around the corner from mediocrity, urging me to stay still and complacent.

It takes courage to step beyond our comfort level. But I've found that risk must be taken, because the greatest hazard in life is to risk nothing. I simply could not learn, feel, change, grow, live or love without risking. Mr. Kershaw was not afraid to venture into dangerous territory. He taught me that in the risking we gain freedom—for ourselves—and sometimes for others too.

Becky psyched herself up to clean Mr. Kershaw's house each week by marching around the shop with her vacuum and mop. "Hut, Two, Three, Four. Forwar-r-r-d. MARCH!" Everyone cleared a path for her as she tramped in, raising and lowering her mop with the proper military bearing. Then, bang! the mop handle would meet the floor with a final, "Company-y-

y-y-y HALT!" Then Becky would click her heels together, stick out her chest and say in a loud deep voice,
"Troops, I'm ready to MOVE OUT!" With a sense of
pride that would bring a tear to a Marine's eye, out she
would go to Mr. Herbert P. Kershaw's house for his
weekly spit and polish.

Becky would catch sight of him as soon as she
turned the corner of his street. There he would be on his
front stairs, back straight, head high, hand to his
forehead in full salute.

"Private McFarland reporting for duty, Sir," she
would say smartly, dragging the equipment out of her
car trunk and up the front stairs.

"At ease, Private," he'd say, dropping the salute and
reaching out his hand to take the vacuum.

"Spot anything suspicious on your way in?" he'd
ask each time.

"No, SIR," Becky would assure him. "The coast is
clear."

The girls at the office referred to Mr. Kershaw as
"touched." Becky called him "Sarge" and didn't mind
the weekly drills one bit because, after all, if it weren't
for men like Sarge, where would this country be? In
fact, she stated, every man in her family fought in a war,
starting from way back when, and were darn proud of
it. So who did they think they were, making fun of old
Sarge, anyway? After one of these patriotic speeches,
the girls would look at each other in agreement: Becky
was well-suited for trench duty.

"Got the tactical support team ready," Mr. Kershaw
barked on Becky's first visit.

"Support team, Sir?"

"You betcha. Right here awaiting orders." And there, sprawled out and fast asleep, was a brown and white blob with a head smooshed into the rug and long floppy ears hanging down on either side. The blob's name was "Grunt"—Sarge's aging bloodhound.

"Great, Sarge," Becky said. "We can use all the help we can get."

More than 50 years earlier, Herbert Kershaw stopped in front of a building to read a poster: "We don't promise you a rose garden."

Without hesitation, he walked in, signed up, and became "One of a few good men." From that very day on, he traveled to exotic places like Parris Island and Twenty-nine Palms; into the Pacific Theatre to Guadalcanal, Tarawa and what was then a sparse, sandy island called Iwo Jima. "Knew Ira Hayes," he announced one day.

"Who?" Becky asked, dusting the pictures on the mantle.

"Crazy Pima Indian. Brave as hell, though. Busted and broken like them other boys, he pushed that flag up straight for the world to see. Took his Medal Of Honor home with him, then got drunk and died on the side of a road in his own vomit. Crazy leatherneck."

Some people in Mr. Kershaw's family thought he was a crazy leatherneck, too, and would brace themselves whenever holiday dinners brought them all together.

"Now, Herbert," his sister Marjorie would say, "it is not polite to wear a hat at the table."

And he'd scowl at Marjorie and say, "If this helmet was good enough to wear on the beach at Iwo Jima, it's good enough to wear at this table, dear sister." And then he would start in about freedom and who fought for it and who didn't and how only the people who were there on the front lines had the right to dictate protocol here or anywhere else. And Semper Fidelis and military stuff like that. And could they all just pass the turkey and quit staring at his helmet?

The young kids loved it. "Hey, Uncle Herbert," they would say after dinner, "tell us about the mountain." And Uncle Herbert would light his pipe and tell them about a remote place called Suribachi.

"Never saw anything like that mountain," he'd begin. "Thought mountains were supposed to be green, covered with lush underbrush and tall trees. This one was like something out of Hades. Something the Devil himself constructed in his hate and fury for mankind."

"We were told it was an extinct volcano. Must have been because it was barren of any living thing. Any living thing, that is, except for the twelve thousand elite troops of the Japanese Imperial Army!

"Nothing prepared us for our first view of this mound of hell called Suribachi. It was barren, all right. A dirty, dusty, almost straight up mountain of volcanic sand. Oh, how deep that sand was. Like trying to move forward in knee-deep snow. Legs burning and muscles straining, me and my boys inched our way up that pile of death. Those Japanese above us on that mountain were watching us every step of the way.

" 'Come on, men,' I'd yell back to my troops. 'Hey, diddle diddle, right up the middle,' I'd say, and up they'd trudge in their sweat-stained green uniforms, weighted down with ammunition belts and bayonets.

'Right behind ya, Sarge,' they'd say, not missing a step."

"Oh, not that we weren't prepared, mind you. Got everyone suited up and briefed real good before we left. We knew they were up there, somewhere, and we were ready for them.

"Just didn't expect to see that grenade rolling down toward us when it did. Wasn't prepared for the detonation or the orange flash that lit up the whole side of that mountain. Took me by surprise when that Japanese metal crashed into my skull and the pain rocketed across my forehead."

"Were you scared, Grandpa?" Timmy, the youngest, asked.

"Not scared exactly, Timmy. Just wasn't expecting to be told that most of my boys were blown apart or that my eyesight was shot for good. They told me I ran back up that mountain blind, screaming like a crazy fool, blasting and bumping into things and cutting down whatever got in my way until someone tackled me and carried me back down off that damn mountain forever. Didn't know I'd be going home so soon."

They would usually take Uncle Herbert home after his story was told and after the children saluted him properly a bunch of times. He was still a hero to them.

He was a worry to Marjorie. "Now, Brother, you do know how I worry. When are you going to get sensible and move out of that house and in with me? It isn't right, you alone here all the time in the dark. Besides, it is so messy. How do you put up with that clutter? There is stuff everywhere. Becky does her best to keep up with it, but there are so many dust collectors."

Those bits of World War II memorabilia may have

seemed like dust collectors to Marjorie, but Becky didn't mind them at all. She liked taking care of the rainbow of ribbons and polishing the medals, stripes and plaques until they were just as shiny as the day Sarge received them. She was fascinated with the old Japanese Samurai sword that hung on the wall, and the faded and tattered Rising Sun flag displayed in the hallway.

She especially liked the large, star-shaped medal in the velvet lined box on the mantle. The one with all the little white stars on it hanging from a light blue ribbon. Mr. Kershaw said that was the one he had traded his eyes for. He said it was presented to him, Gunnery Sergeant Herbert P. Kershaw, United States Marine Corps, by President Franklin D. Roosevelt himself, right there on the lawn of 1600 Pennsylvania Avenue. Bent right down while President Roosevelt slipped the ribbon around his neck. Hanging from that ribbon is the one they call the Congressional Medal of Honor.

When her cleaning was done, Becky would turn to Sergeant Herbert P. Kershaw and say, "Mission accomplished, Sir. Troops are moving out."

Then she would stand at attention, salute and walk away thinking, "That old hero fought hard to preserve our freedom. Now he's entitled to his share."

17

Sweeping Skeletons Out of the Closet

I'd made up my mind early on in the business that my company would be known as the one to count on for dirt elimination, no matter where the dirt showed up. So, off we'd gallop with our cleaning buckets, mops and, sometimes—with mirrors and silver crosses. I learned through those experiences what Susan Jeffers meant when she wrote <u>Feel The Fear and Do It Anyway</u>.

D o you guys believe in ghosts?" I asked the gals at the cleaning shop one day. Tracy and Denise eyed me suspiciously from the desk where they sat folding rags.

"Well," started Tracy, "I always thought ghosts were friendly...until I saw *Poltergeist*."

Denise got up and snuck behind Tracy. "Mom-m-y," she whispered in a little girl's voice. "It's m-e-e-e, Carol Ann, and they're b-a-a-ck."

"Stop it!" shrieked Tracy, twirling around, grabbing for Denise.

"While you two work out your poltergeist theories, I

want to tell you about an interesting job."

"Oh, no," they groaned together.

J. Ellison Kelly, the elderly resident manager of the Sprague Mansion in Cranston, a nearby town, had called for help. The mansion was run by a historical society, but the volunteers were too old to do heavy cleaning. Despite its popularity as a wedding site, the mansion's third floor was rumored to be haunted.

"They need you all tomorrow," I said.

"Not in this lifetime," blurted Tracy. "That place gives me the spooks. I took a tour there once and wandered away from the group into the parlor. I just went over to check out the grand piano in the corner and someone or *something* tapped me on the shoulder."

"Well, tell them we'll consider it if we can bring along some guys," said Denise, winking.

"Like who?" I asked. "Your husbands?"

"Not a chance," said Denise. "I was thinking more along the lines of Dan Aykroyd, Bill Murray and Rick Moranis."

"Who ya gonna call, when ya don't know who to call?" Tracy sang. Everybody yelled out in unison, *"Ghostbusters!"*

I called Mr. Kelly back. "We'll all be there tomorrow." It wasn't my job to keep their minds off apparitions. And besides, I was curious.

"Oh, that's lovely," Mr. Kelly answered softly. "I'll tell the others." I wondered just who the "others" were and thought of the Bates Motel.

The Sprague Mansion was built in 1790 by William Sprague, a textile printer from Salem, Massachusetts.

He moved to Rhode Island, made a fortune and constructed the stately home for his wife and two sons. The mansion was a massive, three-story Colonial affair with vast high ceilings, parquet floors, mahogany staircases, banisters and intricately carved moldings.

When we got to the mansion, I rang the doorbell as Denise made creaking sounds and Tracy giggled, humming the *Ghostbusters* tune.

Mr. Kelly answered the door, written instructions in hand. He was about 65 with horn-rimmed glasses and a nerdy expression that implied a shy, maladjusted blue blood who spent too much time alone. He offered a limp handshake.

"All the wood needs cleaning. Every room, every floor, top to bottom," We unloaded two car trunks filled with supplies: Murphy's Oil Soap to clean and condition the wood, lemon oil to moisturize the wood, liquid wax to polish the wood, butcher's wax to buff it all up and three wooden Indians to do the work: Denise, Tracy and me.

"Let's start upstairs," I suggested. Mr. Kelly started to cough.

"Uh, Mr. Kelly," I asked, "something wrong?"

"No, no, no, no, no," he stuttered, clutching his hands. "It's nothing, oh, nothing at all," he squeaked. "But, uh, perhaps, you could begin on the second floor and save the third floor for last," he said, his voice trailing. I looked at the gals. They looked at Mr. Kelly. Tracy took something out of her back pocket and clenched it in her hand. It slid and clunked on the floor—a thick, silver cross.

"Hey, Trace," Denise teased. "Did you remember the

silver stake, too?"

"Cool it, Denise," I said, shooting her a sharp glance. Mr. Kelly had left. We spread out in the living room, dragging mops and ladders. Tracy stuffed her cross in her back pocket.

Cleaning the first floor was actually quite easy. Part was closed off to visitors and used mostly for storage, so the most frightening creatures we encountered were spiders, dead moths and the shadows of a few buzzing flies.

"See, Trace," Denise said, pulling down the last of the cobwebs, "Told you there was nothing to worry about."

As if on cue, a door slammed shut upstairs. The broom, wrapped with cobwebs like cotton candy, dropped from Denise's hand. "What was that?"

Tracy smiled. "Just your imagination, Denise."

Mr. Kelly, who seemed to have vanished... reappeared. "Please join me for tea. We drink it twice a day here."

We charged into the kitchen, Denise in front, and packed around the table. It seemed a good time to ask him about the rumors.

Some, it turned out, were true. Mr. Sprague had choked to death on a fishbone in this very kitchen. Then, Amasa Sprague, who took over the textile company after his dad's untimely death, was murdered in the backyard by his business associates.

"No need to worry," Mr. Kelly said, (with forced nonchalance, I thought). "The house has been quiet for years."

"But what about the spirit that people talk about?"

Denise asked. "Did it kill anyone?" I realized there were more rumors than I had heard.

"Well, I suppose I should tell you, since you will be cleaning that area. We realized there was a...shall we say...visitor a few years ago when one of our volunteers from the society was cleaning the doll room on the third floor. It was where Mrs. Sprague kept a collection of dolls. Each one needed to be dusted off."

"He was up there for quite a while," he continued, "dusting and cleaning, when all of a sudden we hear this high-pitched yell and a door slammed. The next thing we knew, he was tripping down the stairs, pale as a sheet. A few days later he told us a ghost had come up next to him and was watching him pick up those dolls.

"What did it look like?"

"I don't know. The man died of a heart attack a couple of weeks later."

When we got back to the office, the gals were quiet.

"You can't force me to go back there tomorrow," Tracy said solemnly. My job description doesn't mention cleaning haunted houses."

"You don't know for sure that it's haunted," Denise challenged. "Just because there were a couple of small incidents a hundred years ago..."

"Small incidents! You call the fishbone episode and Amasa's murder small incidents! That's like saying the Titanic bumped into an ice cube! And what about that door slamming upstairs? Thanks anyway, but I'm calling in sick tomorrow. You can clean the Marquis de Sade's torture palace all by yourself." Tracy liked to exaggerate sometimes.

"Tracy," I pleaded, "you guys have got to come back

with me tomorrow. They have a big wedding scheduled for Sunday. You can't drop out now."

"Okay, okay," Tracy said, throwing up her hands. "But I'm not touching the third floor. I don't want to run into Willie or any of his offspring."

I decided to call Mr. Kelly to inquire further.

"I know I promised to clean the house for this wedding, but, to tell you the truth, we are all getting a little edgy about the place. These mysterious deaths—you might as well level with me. Is there anything else?"

"There was one more body," he said. "But I'm late for a society meeting. I'll tell you about him when you get here tomorrow."

As we drove to the mansion the next morning, I decided not to tell Tracy or Denise that Mr. Kelly had more stories. "He said we could skip the third floor."

Let's just finish up with the second floor and we'll be out of there," I chirped.

"Oh, okay. But don't ask me to step foot anywhere else," said Tracy, her pockets bulging. I could only guess what silver trinkets were stuffed there.

We flew through the second floor, washing and polishing like a couple of Charlie Chaplin characters in a film stuck in fast forward.

We packed our rags and were heading downstairs when Denise became adventurous. "This is absurd. We're grownups and we don't have to be afraid of things that aren't real. C'mon, let's check out the third floor."

Tracy reached into her pockets, pulled out the cross and turned around. "I'm out of here," she said, heading down the stairs.

"Well," Denise challenged, looking at me, "are you scared, too?"

I wouldn't have minded following Tracy, but my ego had gotten involved. I was the boss and had to set a mature example. "No big deal," I said.

We peeked downstairs to see Tracy polishing the banister, then looked up the stairs. We waited for them to creak, but they didn't. At the top of the stairs, a hallway veered off to the right, filled with chairs under dusty sheets. We figured we would take that route in case Mr. Kelly gathered his nerve and came up. We tiptoed to the first door and opened it. A bathroom with a broken mirror. The next door seemed unwilling to open, but we pushed it hard and it came off the top hinge.

"Creepy," uttered Denise.

A window near the bed was open and two curtains, which must have been white years ago, blew in the breeze. A dresser nearby stood close to another door.

"I wouldn't mind opening that closet, but I have to get up my nerve," Denise said, plopping down in the dresser chair.

"What are you doing?" I asked, impatient to go.

"Imagining I'm a fancy lady waiting for my servant to comb my hair."

I was going to stand behind her with a make-believe hatchet when I noticed it: a slight opening of the door next to us.

I clutched Denise's shoulder, but she had seen it too.

The door began to open and we both screamed and spun around poised to run out the bedroom door.

"Oh, I'm sorry I frightened you," said Mr. Kelly, who had opened the door to reveal an adjoining bedroom. "I was just looking for you. Tea's ready."

We sat on the mansion porch for the last chapter of the story. Early in the 1930's the house was sold to a Hiram Styron, a society member. After hearing strange sounds for several nights, he invited a friend over who had a Ouija board. They summoned the ghost and asked his identity, thinking it would turn out to be the old man or his son. It turned out to be the butler, Charles, who told them the whole story.

"How did he do that?" Tracy asked.

"They asked the Ouija board. He said that in the late 1800's his daughter was romantically involved with one of the young Sprague men against her father's wishes.

"Well, the men headed up the stairs to the third floor and poked through a boarded entrance in the older part of the home which gave way to the newer addition and into the doll room. The door turned out to connect the servants' quarters with Charles' room."

When he finished, I said, "Let me get this straight. Are you telling us that it isn't Mr. Sprague or any of his family haunting this place? That it was the butler all this time?"

"I am," he stated, coughing a bit.

We drove back to the office in silence, each of us digesting the story and the fact that we had been in a genuine haunted house.

Finally, Tracy looked at me straight in the eye and said, "Let's just keep this a secret between us, okay? No one would ever believe the butler did it."

18

Restoring Faded Slippers

An 85-year-old man who knew he was dying said, "If I had it to do all over again, I'd start barefoot earlier in the spring and stay that way later in the fall. I'd ride more merry-go-rounds, I'd watch more sunrises, and I'd play with more children." Mrs. Avadesian taught me to dance often and begin immediately.

My favorite customer was Mrs. Avadesian. I'm not sure how old she was, but I do know that all her children were on Social Security. I discovered a secret she kept even from them.

It occurred one morning when I lugged a vacuum into her living room. She was holding something in her hands and giggling.

"Oh my," she stammered, backing away sheepishly, her hands behind her back. She was a wiry little Armenian woman given to complaining about the Turks, who, she constantly tried to convince me, had stolen the Armenians' land centuries ago.

I wondered if she held a political flyer.

She paused a moment, then said "Shush," looked around guiltily, and pulled out a faded, 1956 version of *Teen Magazine*. Despite its age, the magazine cover was striking. Smiling at us was none other than Elvis himself! His heavy-lidded eyes smoldered: "I need you now!" I looked at Mrs. Avadesian. Her face was flushed.

"Is he ever hot," I yeowed before thinking better.

"You, too?"

"Are you kidding? I had my first kiss in the back seat of my boyfriend's Fairlane to *'Hold me close, hold me tight, let me thrill with delight...'*" I whirled the vacuum cleaner hose, pressing it close to my neck.

From then on we were a two-person, secret fan club.

Every Wednesday, after I cleaned her house, the King visited Mrs. Avadesian's living room, and we danced.

When she felt extra frisky, she would drag out a pink appliquéd organza dress, which was too big for her birdlike frame, and she would slip into pink satin heels. She would fashion her long, silky gray hair and twist it into a braid, tying it around the top of her head. Often, while I cleaned her other rooms, I would hear her fussing with the Motorola Victrola in the parlor, anticipating my presence. For her birthday, I gave her a somewhat scratched but perfectly usable album of Elvis' Greatest Hits that I had fought for and won at a yard sale.

It was on a Tuesday that her son called to tell me she was in the hospital for chemotherapy. "We hope she'll be okay, but she isn't getting any younger. You might pray for her."

That week I put a candle for Mrs. Avadesian next to a statue of Jesus and nearby leaned a photo of Elvis I clipped from a magazine. If Elvis was around up there, perhaps he could help her out.

Six weeks later, she called to say she was home and could I resume our schedule. I loaded up my supplies and headed over.

She wore a grin on her face, which had paled considerably, and, despite its faded hue, gave off a girlish glow. She had applied makeup: pearl-pink iridescent lipstick, tomato-red cheeks and magenta eye shadow applied in the general vicinity of her lids.

"I'm so glad I'm back," she said excitedly, taking my hand and leading me to the Victrola.

"Are you sure you're ready..."

"Shush. I'm fine," she said, pulling *Jailhouse Rock* from its sleeve. We jitterbugged, with me leading because I was taller and stronger. She twirled and hopped, pink satin slippers gliding over the rug. Elvis was relentless, his fire inextinguishable. "Please, Elvis, *Don't Be Cruel*," we sang. Then we rested for 20 minutes.

For his finalé, the King swore his undying love. I swooped Mrs. Avadesian up in my arms and waltzed her across the floor. Although we usually took turns leading, I could tell she needed to lean on me. *"Love me tender, love me still, never let me go. For my darling I love you. And I always will."*

And he did—every Wednesday morning for all the Wednesdays Mrs. Avadesian had left.

"Prayer and housekeeping, they go together. They have always gone together. We simply know that our daily round is how we live. When we clean and order our homes, we are somehow also cleaning and ordering ourselves."

–GUNILLA NORRIS, *BEING HOME*

Getting our homes in order, spiritually, physically and emotionally, requires continuous soulful uncluttering...having the will to let go of the old to make room for the new. This takes courage because we're used to the old. Who knows what to expect behind a door we've never opened? Adjustments, changes, uncertainty—moving beyond our comfort zone.

Sort of like that old game show where contestants had to choose between three doors, any of which might reveal the grand prize or the booby prize. But in the game of life, I've found that when I "let go and let God" there are no booby prizes, only previously undiscovered treasure.

The most productive periods of my life have been during the "trash can" stages. These were times of upheaval, when life seemed to upchuck all over me, causing me to retreat, reflect, regroup and ultimately, to unclutter.

Getting "dumped *on*" was a tip-off. Something, usually internal litter, needed to be "dumped *off*." That's where the trash cans came in.

Reflective periods always revitalized me. I'd spring

from thoughtfulness right into action. Closets got cleaned out, old files trashed, sock drawers reorganized and trash cans filled, emptied and refilled casting out the old, making room for the new.

Looking back through my first fifty years, I now understand what Charles Dickens meant when he wrote in *A Tale of Two Cities*:

> *"It was the best of times,*
> *it was the worst of times.*
>
> *It was the season of darkness,*
> *it was the season of light."*

And Forest Gump, who wraps it up another way:

> *"Life is like a box of chocolates.*
> *You never know what you're gonna get."*

What I got was a sometimes looney life as a wife, mother, cleaning lady, business owner, singer, writer, human being and spiritual seeker.

You know, it's funny. When I think back over all those roles, they seem like part of a much larger play, staged here on earth, but written and cast by Heavenly directors. None of it seems real at all. My entire life is perhaps just a moment of comic relief in a much larger cosmic sitcom.

Who knows? Certainly not me. All I know for sure is that I've made it this far with one hand holding a mop and the other pressed gently into the hand of God.

There have been times of heartache and hilarity,

belly-laughs and belly-aches. And, as they say, the beat goes on.

When I started menopause, I decided to sell the company, taking along my favorite vacuum and a bucket full of memories.

I also sold the house and the snow shovel, filled and emptied tons of trash cans, loaded up Shirley (who mascarades as a Ford Taurus), and headed to Hollywood—Florida.

Many afternoons now I sit at a sidewalk table painting pottery at Kimberly's studio in Miami Beach. (She thinks I'm painting, but what I'm really doing is watching bare-chested hunks on rollerblades.)

So, I invite you to do some of your own spring cleaning. Check out the places in your heart and soul that may have become crusty, dusty, moth-eaten, or so crammed with stuff from the past that there's no place for anything new. Throw open the windows, let in the light, listen to the laughter, and get ready for new adventures blown in on the breeze.

As for my own future? Who knows? But one thing you can count on. You'll be among the first to know...

Love,

Joy

Do you have a story?

You are invited to contribute a story for the upcoming sequel to *Spring Cleaning for the Soul*.

Do you have an inspiring, funny or entertaining "cleaning" story, article or anecdote from your own life or someone else's?

The purpose of this second book in the *Spring Cleaning* series is to illuminate the dignity, courage and honor of those who serve others and the hilarity involved in dirt removal.

All stories are welcome. They may be original or one of your personal favorites collected from magazines, newspapers or other sources properly credited, of course. Please keep them under 1200 words and feel free to submit more than one story. You will be acknowledged in the book for your contribution if it is selected.

Please mail to Abbondanza!, P.O. Box 220173, Hollywood, FL 33022-0173 or fax to (954) 927-3068.

Thank you for joining me in this Soulful Spring Cleaning adventure.

Joy Krause

Presentations by Joy Krause

Joy Krause uplifts and motivates audiences with humorous, inspirational presentations on change, leadership, values and abundance in her own unique, dynamic and entertaining style.

If you would like to receive a promotional package or contact Joy to set up an event, please call or write:

Joy Krause
Abbondanza!
P.O. Box 220173
Hollywood, FL 33022-0173

Phone: (954) 927-3960 • (800) 791-8799
Fax: (954) 927-3068
E-Mail: SprngClng@aol.com

Order Form

Abbondanza!, P.O. Box 220173
Hollywood, FL 33022-0173
(954) 927-3960

Please send_____copies of *Spring Cleaning for the Soul*
to:

Name_____

Company_____

Address_____

City_____

State_____ Zip_____

Telephone_____

Payment:

Check ❑   included (Payable to Abbondanza!)

VISA ❑   Master Card ❑

Card number:_____

Expiration date:_____

Cardholder Signature_____

Spring Cleaning for the Soul U.S. $ 9.95   _____

Spring Cleaning for the Soul Canada $11.95   _____

    Subtotal   _____

    6.5% Tax (Florida)   _____

    Shipping $2 first book $1 each additional   _____

           TOTAL _____

Toll Free (800) 791-8799

Have your VISA or Master Card ready

Fax Orders: (954) 927-3068

On-line Orders: SprngClng@aol.com

Order Form

Abbondanza!, P.O. Box 220173
Hollywood, FL 33022-0173
(954) 927-3960

Please send_____copies of *Spring Cleaning for the Soul*
to:

Name_____

Company_____

Address_____

City_____

State_____ Zip_____

Telephone_____

Payment:

Check ❑ included (Payable to Abbondanza!)

VISA ❑   Master Card ❑

Card number:_____

Expiration date:_____

Cardholder Signature_____

Spring Cleaning for the Soul U.S. $ 9.95   _____
Spring Cleaning for the Soul Canada $11.95   _____
   Subtotal   _____
   6.5% Tax (Florida)   _____
   Shipping $2 first book $1 each additional   _____
                                 TOTAL _____

Toll Free (800) 791-8799
Have your VISA or Master Card ready
Fax Orders: (954) 927-3068
On-line Orders: SprngClng@aol.com